Hear O Lord
Poems From the Disturbances of 2000–2009

Eliaz Cohen

Hear O Lord

Poems From The Disturbances Of 2000–2009

TRANSLATED BY

Larry Barak

The Toby Press

Hear O Lord
Poems From the Disturbances of 2000–2009

First Hebrew-English Edition, 2010

The Toby Press LLC
POB 8531, New Milford, CT. 06676-8531, USA
POB 2455, London W1A 5WY, England
& POB 4044, Jerusalem 91040, Israel
www.tobypress.com

ISBN 978 159 264 313 4, *paperback original*

A CIP catalogue record for this title is available from the British Library

Typeset by Koren Publishing Services
Printed and bound in Israel

לבני משפחתי, אהובַי
שכולם עִמדי
לא נפקד מהם איש

To my family
my loved ones
who are all with me
not a one is missing

Contents

Introduction to Hear O Lord 1
Translator's Note 9

(close your eyes now) 13
Hear, O Lord 15
News 17
(now I am very sick with love) 19
Tashlich 21
Kislev, on the Way to Hebron 25
Two Poems on Ishmael 31
From Poems of the Mountain Village [a] 33
With Me From Lebanon 37
(And at night) 43
Ultrasound 45
The Land Lost its Way 47
Prayer for the Driver on the Tunnel Road 49
From Poems of the Mountain Village [b] 51
A Spring Journey in the Land of Israel, 5762 55
Draw Me After You 59
A Palestinian Passover 61

THE POET GOES TO WAR

(on the second day) 67
Nablus, We have Returned to You 69
And in Time of War 71
In Nablus I Saw 73
He Who Dreamed 75

Her Sacrifice. 77
Poem On Tel and Not Aviv 85
Snow 89
Here Comes Our Messiah 91
You Will Yet See. 93
Above Ariel. 95
Night in Jerusalem 103
(Sitting on the bus which is ticking). 105
Something Will Rise Yet. 107
(and suddenly spring burst forth in the middle) 109
The Bound Ones 111
Pre-Messianic Pangs 113
Selling Again 115

AN INVITATION TO CRY

An Invitation to Cry. 119
This Land Trembling Under Our Feet. 123
The Death of the Whale 125
Poems Written in the Sand [a] 127
Poems Written in the Sand [b] 131
Poems Written in the Sand [c] 137
In the Margins of the Poems. 141

From Me To My Uncle (a cycle in progress) 143
From Poems of the Coming Holocaust. 149
The Barrier Crasher 153

The Last Ridge 157
(Among the fragments of the bus and your burnt) 159
Waiting, Still 161
(and at night) 167
(when I am close to my death) 169
To Grasp Time by the Hair and Agitate It 171

Notes 173
About the Author 179

Introduction

David C. Jacobson

Born in Petach Tikva in 1972, at the age of seven Eliaz Cohen moved with his religious Zionist family to the West Bank settlement of Elkana. Although his parents were supporters of the Gush Emunim settlement project inspired by Rabbi Zvi Yehuda Kook, they did not bring him up with the rigid ideological purity that characterized other Gush Emunim settlers. Throughout his childhood, Cohen was encouraged to be true to himself and to be wary of being overly influenced by anyone, including the rabbinic teachers in the yeshiva where he studied.

Cohen began his writing career as an author of prose, but eventually he came to focus primarily on poetry. He is an editor of the poetry journal *Mashiv Haruach*, founded in 1994 by a small group of religiously observant Israelis, most of whom either grew up in the territories occupied by Israel in 1967 or were educated there. This bilingual edition of Cohen's poetry is based on his two most recent collections, *Shema Adonai: Mishirei Me'ora'ot 5761–5764* (*Hear O Lord: Poems From the Disturbances of 2000–2004*), 2004, written during the Palestinian uprising known as the Second Intifada, and *Hazmana*

LeBekhi: Shisha Shirim al HaHitnatkut (*An Invitation to Cry: Six Poems on the Disengagement*), 2005, written during the period leading up to Israel's disengagement from Gaza and Northern Samaria.

Cohen aspires in his poetry to transcend the particulars of political conflict, whether between Israelis and Palestinians or among Israelis. The difficult events of these times provided him with occasions for the writing of poetry that deals with the archetypal theological, historical, and psychological issues that have been an integral part of Jewish existence throughout history and of the human condition in general. This poetry runs the gamut from the despair and anger evoked by death and destruction to a celebration of love for his beloved wife Efrat, his precious children, Achia, Oria, Shaked, and Miriam, the Land of Israel, his fellow soldiers who fell in battle, and even for the Palestinian "other." In some poems he goes so far as to assert his belief in the coming of universal peace during the Messianic Era.

Like many Israelis, Eliaz Cohen's family history has been haunted by the human sacrifices that have been the result of the Arab-Israeli conflict. His uncle, Eliezer Feldman, for whom Cohen was named, was killed in battle in the Sinai Campaign of 1956. During Israel's War of Independence in 1948, Cohen's grandparents' cousins were among those who had to flee Gush Etzion when it was conquered by Arab forces. After the Six-Day War in 1967, when Gush Etzion was once again under Israeli control, the son of his grandparents' cousins returned to live in the region from where his parents had fled, but sadly he died fighting in the Yom Kippur War in 1973.

The Second Intifada brought its own measure of suffering to Cohen's generation as well: suicide bombings in buses, restaurants, and other public places; sniper attacks; and military casualties during combat with Palestinian fighters. The existential fears experienced by Cohen during that difficult period permeated his imagination and his subconscious. In one poem, he fantasizes riding in a bus writing his last poem before the bus is blown up by a terrorist. In another poem, he has a nightmare of fighting Palestinians in the West Bank city of Jenin, a hotbed of terrorism, "exposed in the turret / my burning tank above the city of Jenin / carries me galloping in flames."

In a number of poems protesting to God for not protecting

the Jews of Israel from the ravages of Palestinian terrorism, Cohen continues a long tradition of challenges to the divine issued by the biblical figures Abraham and Moses, Honi the Circle Maker of rabbinic legend, and the Hasidic master Levi Yitzhak of Berdichev. In the poem "Hear O Lord," Cohen transforms the first biblical passage of the Shema prayer, in which God commands his people to be loyal to his teachings, into a call to God to be fully aware of the "sons who are being killed for you daily." Similarly, in "Palestinian Passover," Cohen bitterly contrasts God's protection of the Israelites on the night of the killing of the first born in ancient Egypt with the contemporary reality in which all too many Israelis have suffered death. In another poem, he writes that the successes of the Palestinian terror campaign against Israel's civilians raise a serious question about whether God is still honoring the covenant He established with the patriarch Abraham. Transcending the anger and frustration of his poetry protesting God's apparent lack of involvement in the world, Cohen was inspired to write a simple petitionary prayer to God, "Prayer for the Driver on the Tunnel Road," asking for His protection from the frequent Palestinian sniper attacks on the road between Gush Etzion and Jerusalem.

Despite the suffering and anger experienced by Cohen in this time of destruction, he writes often of feelings of love and human empathy that allow him to transcend the hatred and death that is so much a part of Israeli existence. In the poem "In Nablus I Saw," based on his participation in the battle of Nablus fought by Israel in response to the attack on a hotel Passover seder in Netanya in 2002, he reflects compassionately on "the face of the Palestinian girl / clinging to the leg of her father." In addition, in a poem titled "With Me from Lebanon," an ironic allusion to an expression in the love poetry of the Song of Songs, Cohen mourns the loss of fellow Israeli soldiers who died in Lebanon during the period in the early 1990s when he served there.

In poems about the Israeli-Palestinian conflict, Cohen does not shy away from brutally violent images. In "Poems Above Ariel," with bitter irony Cohen invites two prominent Palestinian poets to violate his body: "O my brother poets of Palestine / come to me /

strip me of my uniform / and on my naked body / stripe me." In "Palestinian Passover," Yasir Arafat is portrayed as if he is the biblical Ishmael, "add[ing] another measure / to the bowl of blood," as he prepares "the bread of great affliction / of both nations." In another poem, "a detached black hand in the towers of the mosques [of Jenin] / wants to stab [his] heart with a curved crescent." Sometimes Cohen eroticizes the Israeli-Palestinian conflict as he expresses his longing for a loving intimate relationship with Palestinians. Inspired by his experience growing up with Arab neighbors in Elkana and the biblical vision of Ishmael and Isaac as brothers, Cohen writes about his longings of love for the Arab with which Israel has been so long in conflict. In "Two Poems on Ishmael," the speaker expresses a sensual attraction to Arab boys, whose presence sends him back to a time before Isaac and Ishmael were separated, as they are "running naked, the hills arching / their green torsos to our bodies." An influential part of his childhood memory is captured in "The Barrier Crasher," dedicated to his Arabic teacher Ali Yichya, the first Arab citizen of Israel to serve as a foreign ambassador. As Cohen stands on guard as a soldier at a roadblock in the West Bank, he recalls fondly his experience studying Arabic in Elkana with Ali Yichya, even as he acknowledges his great discomfort at the power imbalance between his position in the Israel Defense Forces and that of the Palestinians over which Israel rules. The poem concludes with the convergence of the Muslim muezzin's call to prayer and the blessing he, as a descendant of the priests of ancient Israel, recites for Arab and Jew alike.

As a second generation religious Zionist settler, Cohen remains committed to the right of Jews to settle throughout the biblical Land of Israel, and he has confirmed that right by living with his wife and children in Kibbutz Kefar Etzion, in the very region from where his grandparents' cousins had fled in 1948. It is therefore not surprising that during the preparation for the disengagement from Gaza and Northern Samaria Cohen expressed his deep involvement in the emotional and spiritual upheaval among religious Zionists at that time. In "Poems Written in the Sand [a]," writing sadly of the vulnerability of the settlement project, he imagines the slogan "The Land of Israel belongs to the people of Israel" written in the sand of the Gaza beach being washed away by a wave from the sea. Of particular concern to Cohen at the time was the painful split in the nation between supporters and opponents of the disengagement and the very difficult position of Israeli soldiers ordered to dismantle Jewish settlements. In "An Invitation to Cry," he imagines his own settlement of Kefar Etzion being subjected to dismantling by the army and the attempts he would make to evoke in a soldier sent to destroy his home some degree of empathy for the suffering of those he was evacuating.

Cohen devoted his first collection of poetry, *Mechumashim* (1997), to modern midrashic responses to the Torah portions read weekly in the synagogue. The sense conveyed in that collection that the present is very much rooted in the past carried over to much of the poetry included in this volume. Indeed, in Cohen's poetic imagination there is often little distinction between his experience as an Israeli Jew and that of his forebears. In "Kislev, on the Way to Hebron," a group of Jews encounters three Arab men who bring to mind the biblical Patriarchs, Abraham, Isaac, and Jacob. Later in that poem, the voice of an Eastern European Hasidic rabbi is suddenly heard: "*yidelach, yidelach*, rise to serve your creator." The biblical story of the binding of Isaac is as relevant today in his modern midrash, "Her Sacrifice" as it ever was. In "With Me from Lebanon," the casualties of contemporary war are compared to the rabbinic martyrs who were victims of Roman persecution, known in the Jewish tradition as "the cedars of Lebanon" (*arzei halevanon*). In "News," a contemporary terrorist attack is announced on the radio, but from Cohen's point of view there is nothing new about Jews suffering: "On the radio they said news / and in our hearts were olds, ancients / and we put our bundles on our shoulders / wedges of cheese, a bread / we returned to our walking." Sometimes the present and the ancient past come together in Cohen's poetry in amusing ways, as in the line "Doing a radio check with God," or when the speaker compares seeing with his wife the ultrasound image of their baby in her womb to the divine revelation at Mount Sinai, in which the Bible relates "all the people saw the sounds."

In defiance of the strict code of sexual modesty prevalent among religiously observant Jews, Cohen has not shied away from erotic imagery in his poetry. In his second collection of poems, *Negi'ot Rishonot* (*First Touchings*, 2000), he wrote of the sexual tension between himself and his wife when they were forbidden by Jewish law to even touch each other before marriage. In poems in this volume, Cohen explores erotic desire and the emotional fulfillment of physical intimacy between a man and a woman within the framework of a committed marriage. In one poem, in language alluding to images from the love poetry of the Song of Songs, the speaker is "very sick with love" and "desiring to enter the locked garden" of erotic pleasure. In another poem, the speaker finds comfort from the pain of history in his beloved: "and at night / when you are spread out before me like a fan / you will hear my arousing cry / and a lamentation and a dirge...." From Cohen's point of view, marital relations are intertwined with the relations of a married couple to their children. In one poem, the speaker hides poems "in the secret parts" of his wife's body, with the expectation that in the morning, "the children will come in under the covers / and find the poems." Furthermore, even in the midst of military service to the nation, Cohen insists on preserving in his consciousness his bonds of love with the members of his family. He expresses this strong commitment to his family when in the poem "And in Time of War" he subversively changes the statement in Maimonides' code of law that a soldier should not think about his wife and children, lest he be distracted from the battle, to an insistence that each soldier should "think of his wife and his sons and his daughter...for his heroism is for them too / and when he returns in peace to the heart of the great embrace / shall he return."

These poems are permeated with Cohen's love of the Land of Israel in general and the Gush Etzion region where he lives in particular. In "A Spring Journey in the Land of Israel 2002," although in his heart he feels the despair of autumn, his emotions are lifted as "here in the orchards of Etzion all is filled with hope / with the blossoming of the cherry trees." Cohen's poems are filled with images of nature that he has observed throughout his travels in Israel: "vines on the terrace," "golden mushrooms among the pines," "boulders growing out of the earth," "the fragrance of a field," "a birch blooming," "flowers strik[ing] the nostrils."

Tossed back and forth between the pain of death and the longing for love, in some poems Cohen finds the strength to hope for a better time, perhaps even for the universal peace that the Jewish tradition promises will arrive during the Messianic Era. In "Snow," birds find footprints in freshly fallen snow in Jerusalem that may be those of the Messiah about to enter the Old City's Gate of Mercy. In "From Poems of the Mountain Village [b]," Cohen declares that when "a noisy crowing from the chicken coops / blurs the dove-like cooing of the Shekhina," he knows that "the redeemer is coming." And in another poem, he declares his faith that "Something will rise yet from all this blood / I see / the crimson garment of the Messiah rising."

Eliaz Cohen does not confine his role in society to that of a poet. He is deeply committed to combating the many social issues that beset Israel, as a professional social worker, a public advocate for social equality, and an outspoken critic of the Israeli rabbinic establishment. This edition of poetry by Eliaz Cohen provides readers with the fortunate opportunity to experience the literary artistry of a most impressive poet, fighter for social justice, religious gadfly, and dreamer of peace.

David C. Jacobson is Professor of Judaic Studies at Brown University. He is author of *Modern Midrash: The Retelling of Traditional Jewish Narratives by Twentieth-Century Hebrew Writers*; *Does David Still Play Before You? Israeli Poetry and the Bible*; *Creator, Are You Listening? Israeli Poets on God and Prayer*; and *Beyond Political Messianism: The Poetry of Second Generation Religious Zionist Settlers.*

Translator's Note

Translating poetry is always a challenge, as one would expect. However, the poetry of Eliaz Cohen presents some special problems. For one thing, it tends to mix various levels of diction ranging from the biblical to military slang, even in the same poem. One will find an occasional Arabic or Yiddish word as well. It is also very rich in allusions. Here also the range is very broad, including quotations from the Bible, references to modern Hebrew poetry, and even bits from popular Israeli songs. Needless to say, many of these allusions will be more familiar to the Israeli reader than to the American or British reader.

The title poem is, of course, based on a passage from the Bible which has become the most famous prayer in the Jewish liturgy. Cohen takes the original text – "Hear, O Israel" – and reverses its direction, defiantly challenging the deity with the cry: "Hear, O Lord." He calls for God to pay heed to the sufferings of Israel his people, with reference to the Holocaust (phosphorescent blue numbers) as well as to the modern day terrorist attacks (the sniper's shot). God may be approached in such a manner without heresy only by a devoutly religious man, one who has a true familiarity with God.

Understandably, the sacrifice of Isaac has become a major theme in Hebrew poetry in general, and the poetry of Eliaz Cohen is no exception. The poem "Her Sacrifice" actually quotes the story of the sacrifice directly from the Bible, while breaking up the text into short passages on which the poet expands from the viewpoint of Sarah, Isaac's mother, in the style of a midrash. In addition to this poem, the theme of the sacrifice of Isaac recurs many times throughout the book.

Another Biblical source which pervades the poetry of Cohen is "The Song of Songs" (Canticles). Often the poet gives an ironic twist to the source, as when he transposes "with me from Lebanon" from its love poem context to the gory battle scenes of the Lebanese War. So many passages from this book have been set to music in Israel and have indeed become quite popular songs that they are likely to be recognized by the Israeli reader even if his knowledge of Biblical literature is not very extensive.

Cohen's poetry contains many other allusions to sources which may be less familiar, such as the books of Isaiah and Jeremiah. When to provide the reader with notes is never an easy question. The Hebrew text, which was published as a book five years ago, appeared virtually without notes. This does not mean that the poetry presented no difficulties for the reader, but rather that the conscientious reader could be expected to overcome many of the difficulties with some effort on his part. This is, after all, the age of Wikipedia. The objective of the notes to this edition is to help the non-Israeli reader with some of the specifically Jewish or Israeli references which, although likely to be familiar to an Israeli reader, may seem esoteric to him – such as Hebrew dates and their significance and certain geographical and historical or topical references. In any case an effort has been made not to over-explain, to keep the notes unobtrusive.

Larry Barak

Larry Barak was born in Chicago in 1942 to Russian immigrant parents with Hasidic roots. As a student of English at Roosevelt University, he won first prize for poetry in the Charles F. McElroy Literary

Contest. After receiving his B.A., he continued his poetry studies in the M.A. program of the Graduate School of the University of Illinois at Chicago Circle.

In 1969, Barak moved to Israel with his wife, settling in Kibbutz Lavi where he has been living ever since. His prize-winning poem in the Ruben Rose Poetry Contest led to his joining the Voices group of Israeli poets writing in English.

As well as writing poetry in both Hebrew and English, he is also an accomplished poetry translator, his translations appearing in various literary publications.

עַכְשָׁו תַּעַצְמוּ אֶת הָעֵינַיִם
דַּמְיְנוּ:

דָּבָר מִכָּל זֶה לֹא קָרָה
בַּעַת־לַיְלָה אוּלַי הֲזָיָה
זֶה מַה שֶּׁזֶּה הָיָה
פְּרִי מֹחוֹ הַמְשׁוֹרֵר
שֶׁל הַקּוֹדֵחַ

דָּבָר מִכָּל זֶה לֹא קָרָה

[וְלֹא עָלוּ הָאֶלֶף בִּסְעָרָה]

וְעַכְשָׁו פִּקְחוּ אֶת הָעֵינַיִם חֲזָרָה

close your eyes now
imagine:

none of this happened
a night phobia perhaps a hallucination
that's what it was
the fruit of the feverish
poet-mind

none of this happened

(and the thousand did not ascend in a storm)

now open your eyes again

שְׁמַע אֲדֹ־נָי

(ייחוד לימים נוראים)

שְׁמַע אֲדֹ־נָי, יִשְׂרָאֵל עַמֶּךָ יִשְׂרָאֵל אֶחָד

וְאָהַבְתָּ אֶת יִשְׂרָאֵל עַמֶּךָ
בְּכָל לְבָבְךָ
וּבְכָל נַפְשְׁךָ
וּבְכָל מְאֹדֶךָ
וְהָיוּ הַבָּנִים הָאֵלֶּה אֲשֶׁר נֶהֱרָגִים עָלֶיךָ כָּל הַיּוֹם
עַל לְבָבְךָ
וְשִׁנַּנְתָּם בִּרְקִיעֶיךָ
וְדִבַּרְתָּ בָּם:
בְּשִׁבְתְּךָ בְּבֵיתֶךָ
וּבְלֶכְתְּךָ בַּדֶּרֶךְ
וּבְשָׁכְבְּךָ וּבְקוּמֶךָ
וּקְשַׁרְתָּם לְאוֹת עַל
יָדֶךָ (סְפָרוֹת כְּחֻלּוֹת זַרְחָנִיּוֹת) וְהָיוּ לְטֹטָפוֹת בֵּין
עֵינֶיךָ (כְּמוֹ פְּגִיעַת הַצַּלָּפִים)
וּכְתַבְתָּם (בְּדָם) עַל־מְזֻזוֹת בֵּיתֶךָ
וּבִשְׁעָרֶיךָ

Hear, O Lord

(prayer for days of awe)

Hear, O Lord, Israel, your people, Israel is one

And you shall love Israel your people
With all your heart
And with all your soul
And with all your might
And these sons who are being killed for you daily shall be
upon your heart
And you shall teach them diligently in your heavens
And you shall talk of them:
When you sit in your house
And when you walk by the way
And when you lie down and when you rise
And you shall bind them as a sign upon
your hand (phosphorescent blue numbers) and they shall be as frontlets
between your eyes (like the sniper's shot)
And you shall write them (in blood) on the doorposts of your house
And on your gates

חֲדָשׁוֹת

בַּחֲדָשׁוֹת בָּרַדְיוֹ אָמְרוּ
שׁוּב פָּגְעוּ בַּכִּסּוּפִים
וְאִשָּׁה אַחַת מָצְאָה אֶת מוֹתָהּ
(שֶׁעַד עַתָּה הָיָה אוֹבֵד בַּגֵּאָיוֹת)

*

עוֹד אָמְרוּ:
בִּישִׁיבַת הַמֶּמְשָׁלָה יָדוּנוּ בִּרְעִידוֹת הָאֲדָמָה שֶׁעֲלוּלוֹת
(וְלֹא חָשִׁים אֵיךְ הָאָרֶץ כְּבָר רוֹעֶדֶת)

*

כַּדּוּר תּוֹעֶה מְחַפֵּשׂ כְּתֹבֶת רַכָּה
רָאִיתִי אִישׁ מְבַקֵּשׁ אַחִים בְּדֶרֶךְ אֲרֻכָּה
בָּרֹאשׁ הָאָנָלִיטִי נוּרָה אֲדֻמָּה מִזְּמַן נִדְלְקָה
מֶזֶג הָאֲוִיר יָבוֹא בּוּקָה מְבֻלָּקָה

*

הַיָּם יִהְיֶה נוֹחַ כְּשֶׁנַּגִּיעַ אֵלָיו
בְּלֹא כֹּחַ.
זֶהוּ סוֹף הַחֲדָשׁוֹת.

*

בָּרַדְיוֹ אָמְרוּ חֲדָשׁוֹת
וּבַלֵּב הָיוּ יְשָׁנוֹת נוֹשָׁנוֹת
וְלָקַחְנוּ אֶת הַפֶּקְלָךְ עַל שֶׁכֶם
חֲרִיצֵי גְּבִינָה, אֶחָד לֶחֶם
שַׁבְנוּ לָלֶכֶת

חורף תשס"א

News

The news on the radio said
another terrorist attack at the Kisufim
and a woman met her death
(which until now was lost in the valleys)

*

they also said:
at the government meeting they will discuss the threat of earthquakes
(unaware that the earth is already trembling)

*

a wayward bullet is searching for its soft address
I saw a man seeking brothers all along the way
in the analytical mind a red light went on long ago
the weather will come in desolation and ruin

*

the sea will be calm when at length we reach it
with depleted strength.
And that's the end of the news.

*

on the radio they said news
and in our hearts were olds, ancients
and we put our bundles on our shoulders
wedges of cheese, a loaf of bread
        we returned to our walking

winter 5761

*

עַכְשָׁו אֲנִי חוֹלֶה מְאֹד בָּאַהֲבָה
שֶׁהִיא גַּעְגּוּעִים
כָּל הַגּוּף נִמְלָא בַּכְּאֵבִים שֶׁל
מֵיתָרִים הַמְבַקְשִׁים לְהִפָּרֵט

עַכְשָׁו אֲנִי חוֹלֶה מְאֹד בָּאַהֲבָה
לֹא רַק אֵיבַר הָאַהֲבָה
(שֶׁהוּא הַלֵּב)
מוּצָף דַּם עִנְּבֵי תְּשׁוּקָה עַד לְהִתְפַּקֵּעַ
גְּרוּרוֹת פּוֹשְׁטוֹת בַּכֹּל כַּשָּׂרִיגִים
רוֹצוֹת לָבוֹא בְּגַן נָעוּל

עַכְשָׁו אֲנִי חוֹלֶה מְאֹד.

*

now I am very sick with love
        which is longing
the entire body fills with the pain of
        strings asking to be strummed

now I am very sick with love
        not only the love organ
        (which is the heart)
is flooded to bursting with the blood of the grapes of lust
        cancerous growths are spreading everywhere like tendrils
        desiring to come into the locked garden

now I am very sick.

תַּשְׁלִיךְ

א.
כְּמוֹ הַחֲצָבִים
הֵם עָמְדוּ שָׁם
בּוֹקְעִים בַּהֲמוֹן עַמּוּדֵי תִּפְרַחַת
בְּגֵי בֶן הִנּוֹם
בַּחֹרֶף הֵם פְּקַעַת אַחַת
בְּגֵי הִנּוֹם
פַּעַם
הֵם לֵב אֶחָד
פְּרָחִים צְעִירִים מְקֻרָבִים אֱלֵי אֵשׁ
נֶעֱקָדִים

ב.
בָּאנוּ דַּרְכָּם
מִתְוַדִּים
כּוֹפְפִים עַמּוּדֵי תִּפְרַחַת גֵּאִים
עַל נִצֵּנוּ
עַל עֲווֹנוֹתֵינוּ
עֲווֹנוֹתַי רַבּוּ מִשַּׂעֲרוֹתַי
הַכִּיסִים נִדְמִים כְּבֵדִים פִּתְאֹם
בָּאנוּ אֵלֶיהָ

ג.
בָּאנוּ לַנִּקְבָּה
כִּמְעַט שֶׁבָּאנוּ בָּהּ
וְאַתְּ אָמַרְתְּ

Tashlich

a.
like the chatzav
they stood there
erupting into many flowering stalks
        in Gai Ben Hinom
in winter they are a single bulb
        in Gai Hinom
at times
they are a single heart
young flowers sacrificed toward fire
        bound

b.
we came by way of them
confessing
bending proud flowering stalks
to our quarrel
to our transgressions
my transgressions more numerous than my hairs
        the pockets suddenly seem heavy
we came to it

c.
        we came to the tunnel
    we almost came inside it
and you said

בּוֹא נְרַכֵל מְעַט
אַחַר כָּךְ
נוּכַל לְהִפָּטֵר מֵחֵטְא
מִמֵּילָא
מְלַכְלָךְ פֹּה כָּל כָּךְ

ד.

וְהִשְׁלַכְנוּ אוֹתָם
חוֹצְבִים מְנַקְּבִים בָּהּ
בַּנִּקְבָּה
בְּהַלְמוּת פַּטִּישֵׁי פִּשְׁעֵינוּ
שָׁמַעְנוּ אָז
גַּם מִן הָעֵבֶר הַשֵּׁנִי
חוֹצְבִים
פִּשְׁעִים נוֹקְשִׁים
עֲרֵבִים זֶה בָּזֶה
וְיָדַעְנוּ
כִּי תַּם עֲמָלֵנוּ.

ה.

מַעְפִּילִים
אַתְּ וַאֲנִי וְהַנַּעַר
בְּנֵי יִשְׁמָעֵאל מַשְׁחִיזִים שַׁבְרִיּוֹת
מְעֻקָּלוֹת כַּחֲצִי סַהַר
מָחָר יֵעָקֵד בְּנֵנוּ
אֲנַחְנוּ שְׁנֵינוּ
נוֹבִיל אוֹתוֹ אֶל הַר

וְשָׁם יֵרָאֶה

let's gossip a little
   afterwards
      we can shed the sin
   in any case
it's so dirty here

d.
and we cast them away
      hewing and piercing in it
      in the tunnel
pounding with the hammers of our sins
      we heard then
from the other side too
      hewing
sins striking
      intermingling
and we knew
      our work was finished.

e.
      ascending
you and I and the boy
sons of Ishmael are sharpening shabria knives
      curved like the crescent moon
tomorrow our son will be sacrificed
   the two of us
will lead him to a mountain

      and there He will appear

כִּסְלֵו, בַּדֶּרֶךְ לְחֶבְרוֹן

בַּדֶּרֶךְ לְחֶבְרוֹן עָצַרְנוּ
בַּמְּעָרָה
הַגְּפָנִים בַּטֶּרָסָה מֵעָל שָׁכְבוּ נְדָפִים וַעֲיָרְמִים
וְאָנוּ נִסְתַּרְנוּ מִפְּנֵי הָרוּחַ הָרָעָה
שֶׁעָבְרָה עַכְשָׁו עַל הָאָרֶץ
עוֹנַת הַמָּסִיק הָיְתָה אָז
וְהַזָּקֵן הֶעֱמִיס שַׂקִּים שַׂקִּים שֶׁל זֵיתִים
שְׁחוֹרִים וִירֻקִּים מְנַטְּפִים שֶׁמֶן מָרִיר
הָיִיתִי בְּאוֹתוֹ הַלַּיְלָה, וְתָאֵב.
בַּבְּקָרִים הָיִינוּ מְלַקְּטִים זְהַב הַפִּטְרִיּוֹת
מִבֵּין לָאֳרָנִים, מִתְקַדְּמִים אֵלֶיהָ מְעַט,
מְעַט טִפַּסְנוּ עַל הָעֵצִים הָעַתִּיקִים
כַּמָּה הַרְפַּתְקָאוֹת שֶׁהֵם עָבְרוּ, גַּם
אֲנַחְנוּ הָיִינוּ לַעֲנָפִים

שׁוּב בַּלַּיְלָה נִמְסָקִים אֶל
בֵּית־הַבַּד, בַּמְּעָרָה.
זָקֵן שֵׁנִי כְּהֵה עֵינַיִם גִּשֵּׁשׁ בְּמַקֵּל חָרוּב
עִמָּנוּ יָשַׁב
יָמִים, אוֹ עָשׂוֹר, לֹא יָדַעְתִּי כַּמָּה
עַד שֶׁנֶּעְלַם

יוֹם יוֹם, עֲטוּרִים תְּפִלִּין בָּלוֹת עִם שֶׁמֶשׁ
הָיִינוּ מִתְקַדְּמִים טֶפַח, וְשָׁבִים
טְפָחַיִם
דְּמֻיּוֹת זְקֵנִים רָאִינוּ בַּיָּרֵחַ הַמִּתְמַלֵּא

Kislev, on the Way to Hebron

On the way to Hebron we stopped
at a cave
the vines on the terrace above lay scattered and bare
and we took cover from the wicked wind
that passed over the land now
it was the harvest season then
and the old man was loading sack after sack of olives
black ones and green ones dripping oil bitter
I was that night, craving.
In the mornings we would gather golden mushrooms
among the pines, advancing a bit,
we climbed the ancient trees sometimes
how many adventures they have had, we
too became branches

again at night harvested to
the olive press, in the cave.
A second old man, dim-eyed, groping with a carob tree stick
sat with us for
days, or a decade, I knew not how long
until he disappeared

day by day, adorned with worn out *tefillin* at sunrise
we would advance one step, and
retreat two
seeing figures of old men in the waxing moon

אֱלֹהִים שׁוֹקֵעַ וְשׁוּב עוֹלֶה
לְמָחֳרָת

"אֵיפֹה אַתָּה אֱלֹהִים" – צָעַקְנוּ
וּמִכָּל הַגֵּאָיוֹת נִתְגַּלְגְּלוּ הֵדִים.
בַּלֵּילוֹת הָיִינוּ הוֹלְכִים וּמִתְנַבְּאִים.
פְּעָמִים הִרְגַּשְׁנוּ קְרוֹבִים מְאֹד אֵלָיו.
בְּי"ט כִּסְלֵו גְּאוּלִים חַגְנוּ סָבִיב
לַמְּעָרָה
מְרַקְּדִים הָיִינוּ בִּרְחִיפָה, מְנַתְּקִים
כַּפּוֹת רַגְלַיִם קָשׁוֹת וּרְטֻבּוֹת מִן
הַסְּלָעִים.

בַּלַּיְלָה נִבְלַעְנוּ בְּכוּכֵי הַמְּעָרָה
יָשַׁנּוּ כָּל כָּךְ חָזָק עַד שֶׁ
לִפְנוֹת בֹּקֶר שָׁרוּ לָנוּ רוּחוֹת בְּתוֹךְ הָאָזְנַיִם
"יִידָעלָךְ, יִידָעלָךְ, קוּמוּ לַעֲבוֹדַת הַבּוֹרֵא"
וְיָדַעְנוּ כִּי רַבֵּנוּ
לִמֵּד גַּם הָרוּחוֹת לָשִׁיר
הָאָרֶץ עֲזוּבָה בְּאֵין עָמָל, וְאֶת אַהֲבוֹת הַצָּהֳרַיִם
נָתַנּוּ
בַּשּׁוֹמֵרוֹת הַחֲרֵבוֹת.
הָאַלּוֹנִים בָּכוּ אֵלֵינוּ כְּשֶׁקָּרַבְנוּ
אֶל הָעִיר
נִגְלָה לְעֵינֵינוּ זָקֵן שְׁלִישִׁי
צוֹלֵעַ לִקְרָאתֵנוּ עַל יְרֵכוֹ
רָאִינוּ
וְהִנֵּה עוֹרוֹ חָלָק כְּנַעַר
וְהוּא מְחַלֵּל בְּקָנֶה דַּק וּמְנֻקָּב

God sets and rises again
the next day

"where are you, God" – we shouted
and echoes rolled through all the ravines.
At night we would go prophesying.
At times we felt very close to Him.
On the 19th of Kislev redeemed we circled
the cave
dancing we hovered detaching hard wet feet from
the rocks.

At night we were swallowed into the nooks of the cave
we slept so deeply when
at dawn winds sang to us in our ears
"*yidelach*, *yidelach*, rise to serve your creator"
and we knew that our Rabbi
taught the winds to sing too
the land is deserted for lack of labor, and our mid-day loving
we did
in the ruined watchmen's huts.
The oaks wept to us when we approached
the city
a third old man came into view
limping toward us
we saw him
and behold his skin was smooth as a young girl's
and he was playing a thin flute carved from cane

וְהַכְּבָשִׂים
הָיוּ פְּזוּרוֹת בַּוָּאדִי
כְּמוֹ סִירוֹת קוֹצָנִיּוֹת.

גַּם כַּאֲשֶׁר קָרַב אֵלֵינוּ
לֹא יָכֹלְנוּ לְהַסְבִּיר כֵּיצַד
הִנְחִית עַל רָאשֵׁינוּ אֶת הֶחָלִיל
וְהוֹצִיא מִכָּל אֶחָד מֵאִתָּנוּ נְחִילִים
נְחִילִים נוֹשְׂאֵי שׁוֹפָר וְלַפִּידִים
בָּאנוּ

לִכְבֹּשׁ הָאַרְמוֹן הַפְּנִימִי וְהַהֵיכָלוֹת

and the sheep
were scattered in the wadi
like thorny shrubs.

Even when he came close to us
we could not explain how
the flute landed on our heads
releasing from each of us swarms
swarms bearing a *shofar* and torches
    we came

to conquer the inner palace and the temples

שְׁנֵי שִׁירִים עַל יִשְׁמָעֵאל

*

יִשְׁמָעֵאל מְיַדֶּה בִּי אֲבָנִים
"מִלִּים"
הוּא צוֹעֵק
מִלִּים קָשׁוֹת מֵאֲבָנִים, וְאֵיפֹה הָיִיתָ
כְּשֶׁגֵּרְשׁוּ אוֹתִי עִם שַׁחַר וְחֵמַת מַיִם
הַבָּנִים שֶׁלָּנוּ
צוֹעֵק יִשְׁמָעֵאל
יִתְרוֹצְצוּ בְּקִרְבֵּנוּ יַעַבְדוּ זֶה לָזֶה
יִשְׂאוּ סֻלָּמוֹת, מַלְאָכִים, נָשִׁים
יְיַדּוּ זֶה בָּזֶה זִכְרוֹנוֹת

*

נְעָרִים עַרְבִיִּים עוֹשִׂים לִי אֶת זֶה
זוֹרְקִים אוֹתִי שְׁלֹשֶׁת אֲלָפִים שְׁבַע מֵאוֹת שָׁנָה
אֲחוֹרָה
רָצִים עֵירֻמִּים, הַגְּבָעוֹת מְקַשְּׁתוֹת
גֵּוָן הַיָּרֹק לְגוּפֵנוּ
אִמּוֹתֵינוּ דָּשׁוֹת מִנְחַת קְנָאוֹת, כְּמוֹ לֹא רוֹאוֹת
כְּשֶׁיִּשְׁמָעֵאל וַאֲנִי זוֹרְעִים בְּרוּחוֹת הַשָּׁמַיִם

Two Poems on Ishmael

*

Ishmael is hurling stones –
"Words" he shouts –
at me
words harder than stones, and where were you
when they drove me away at dawn with a flask of water
our sons
Ishmael cries
will jostle within us will serve each other
will conjoin with ladders, angels, women
will hurl at each other memories

*

Arab boys do it to me
they throw me three thousand seven hundred years
back
running naked, the hills arching
their green torsos to our bodies
our mothers thresh an envy offering, unawares
while Ishmael and I are sowing the winds of heaven

מִשִּׁירֵי הַכְּפָר שֶׁבָּהָר [א]

א.
כָּאן חַיַּי
בְּבֵיתִי אֲשֶׁר כָּרִיתִי לִי
בָּהָר

ב.
הָיִיתִי הוֹלֵךְ
וּפָנַי מוּל הָרוּחַ
מִן הָרוּחוֹת הַמִּתְקַדְּשׁוֹת שֶׁל
גּוּשׁ עֶצְיוֹן
כָּל בָּתֵּי הָאֶבֶן כְּמוֹ
סְלָעִים צוֹמְחִים מִתּוֹךְ הָאֲדָמָה
מְצַמְּחִים עֻבְרֵי סֶלַע
יְלָדִים שֶׁל אֶבֶן.
אֲנִי, אֵינֶנִּי שֶׁל אֶבֶן, אֲנִי
עַל כֵּן הַכֹּל נִרְשָׁם בִּי

ג.
כְּשֶׁעֲשַׁן הַקִּיטוֹר שָׁחוֹר מִדַּי
אֲנִי נִמְלָט אֶל
בֵּית הַמִּדְרָשׁ
שָׁף אֶת עֵינַי
בִּשְׁנֵי קוּרִים דַּקִּים שֶׁל כֶּסֶף

From Poems of the Mountain Village [a]

a.
my life is here
in my house which I dug
in the mountain

b.
I would walk
my face against the wind
one of the hallowed winds
of Gush Etzion
all the stone houses are like
boulders growing out of the earth
raising rock fetuses
children of stone.
I am not of stone, not I,
that is why in me all is recorded

c.
when the column of smoke becomes too black
I escape to
the study hall
rub my eyes
with two thin webs of silver

ד.

בָּאתִי אֶל בֵּית הַמִּדְרָשׁ
שָׁם
שְׁתֵּי לֶהָבוֹת
קוּרִים שֶׁל כֶּסֶף דַּק מִטַּמְּרִים
הַכֹּל נֶעֱקָדִים פֹּה, בָּהָר
לוֹחֲשׁוֹת הַשַּׁלְהָבוֹת שֶׁל כֶּסֶף
נִכְנָס שָׁלוֹם קַרְנִיאֵל*
בָּא, נִתְיַשֵּׁב לְיָדִי
רוֹצֶה לִכְתֹּב שִׁיר בְּחַבְרוּתָא
וְיָדוֹ מְרַחֶפֶת מֵעַל שֶׁלִּי
כִּמְעַט אוֹנֶסֶת אוֹתָהּ לִכְתֹּב
דְּבָרִים אוֹפְּטִימִיִּים
אִי־אֶפְשָׁר לִכְתֹּב שִׁירִים בְּחַבְרוּתָא
אֲנִי אוֹמֵר לוֹ
וְהוּא מִתְפּוֹגֵג

ה.

בַּחֲדַר הָאֹכֶל
לְעֵת עֶרֶב
אֲנִי רוֹאֶה שֶׁפָּם מְחַיֵּךְ
מְבָרֵךְ עַל הַלֶּחֶם הַחַם
"בָּרוּךְ אַתָּה אֲדֹ־נָי
הַמּוֹצִיא לֶחֶם מִן הַסֶּלַע"
וְרוּחוֹת מִזְדַּקְּנוֹת שׁוֹרְקוֹת אַחֲרָיו:
אָמֵן סֶלַע, אָמֵן סֶלַע

* שלום קרניאל הי"ד, משורר ומחנך, מחלוצי כפר עציון תש"ג–תש"ח. נפל בקרב "שיירת העשרה", כסלו תש"ח.

d.
I came to the study hall
there
two flames
webs of thin silver are billowing
everyone is bound on the altar here, on the mountain
the flames of silver whisper
Shalom Karniel* enters
approaches, sits next to me
wants us to write a poem jointly
and his hand hovers over mine
almost coercing it to write
optimistic things
it's impossible to write poems jointly
I tell him
and he dissipates

e.
in the dining room
at evening
I see a smiling mustache
say the blessing over the warm bread
"Blessed art Thou, O Lord,
who brings forth bread from the rock"
and the aging winds whistle after him:
amen selah, amen rock

* Shalom Karniel, poet and educator, one of the pioneer settlers of the original Kfar Etzion, fell in the battle of "the Convoy of Ten" in Kislev, 5708.

אִתִּי מִלְּבָנוֹן

(פואמת זיכרון)

כָּל אֶחָד יֵשׁ לוֹ אֶת הַלְּבָנוֹן שֶׁלּוֹ
חַיָּל יָפֶה הָרוּג נִשָּׂא עַל הַכְּתֵפַיִם
הֵבֵאתִי
אִתִּי מִלְּבָנוֹן.
שְׁמוֹתָיו מְמַלְמְלִים אֵלַי לֹא אֶרְצֶה לִזְכֹּר
פָּנָיו

כָּל אֶחָד יֵשׁ לוֹ אֶת הַלְּבָנוֹן שֶׁלּוֹ
שֶׁרֶט בַּנֶּפֶשׁ
אֲנִי זוֹכֵר רַק אֶת הַסְּלָעִים, הָעֲלִיָּה
מ ת
נ שף נוֹפֵל עַל הַקּוֹצִים וְהוּא עָלַי וְהוּא
אִתִּי מִלְּבָנוֹן

יוֹאָב.
בַּבְּקָרִים, טְפִיחוֹת קַלּוֹת מֵעִיר אֶת חַיָּלָיו.
מַשְׁחִיז קָצֶה שֶׁל עִפָּרוֹן, עַל דַּף חָלָק נִרְשָׁם עוֹלָם עַכְשָׁו:
פָּנִים שֶׁנִּדְרְכוּ, אַיִל נֶאֱחָז בָּעֵץ הַמְּלֻבְלָב.
אָבָק וְרֵיחַ דָּם עוֹלִים מִמַּאֲרָב.
הוּא מֵת יָפֶה, יוֹאָב.
נְקֻדָּה בַּמֵּצַח, כְּמוֹ נַעֲרָה הֹדִית מְיֹעֶדֶת לְאִישׁ לֹא פְּגָעוּ
בַּנְּמָשִׁים הַגּוּף עוֹד הִמְשִׁיךְ לְהִסְתָּעֵר כְּמוֹ פִּנְתֵּר
וּלְבָנוֹן אִתִּי אֵין דֵּי בַּעַר
כָּל אֶחָד יֵשׁ לוֹ אֶת הַלְּבָנוֹן שֶׁלּוֹ

With Me From Lebanon

(A MEMORIAL POEM)

Every one has his own Lebanon
a handsome dead soldier carried on my shoulders
I brought
with me from Lebanon.
His names mumble to me I do not want to remember
        his face

every one has his own Lebanon
a scratch on his soul
I remember only the rocks, the ascent
                                        Br ea th
ing hard falling on the thorns and he upon me and he
with me from Lebanon

Yoav.
At morning, a light tapping waking his soldiers.
Sharpening the end of a pencil, on a blank sheet of paper a world is
        recorded now:
        tensed faces, a ram caught in the green tree.
Dust and the smell of blood rising from an ambush.
        He died handsome, Yoav.
A spot on his forehead, like an Indian girl promised to a man they
        did not harm
the freckles the body continued to attack like a panther
and Lebanon with me is not sufficient to burn

Every one has his own Lebanon

עֲבָר גָּדֵל דּוֹקֵר
שֶׁתִּזָּכֵר!

פְּתַח לְבָנוֹן דְּלָתֶיךָ וְיָבוֹאוּ כָּל חַיָּלַי
הַמְכֻנָּפִים הַמְהֻזִּים
וְיִנָּטְעוּ בְּךָ כַּאֲרָזִים.
כְּמוֹ יוֹאָב כְּמוֹ
נָדָב.

מַרְאֵהוּ כַּלְּבָנוֹן וּמִי שֶׁאֵרַשׂ אִשָּׁה וְלֹא לְקָחָהּ עִמּוֹ בְּלַהַב
אֵשׁ רוֹצֶה לִצְעֹק אִתִּי
מִלְּבָנוֹן כַּלָּה אִתִּי
מִלְּבָנוֹן תָּבוֹאִי
תִּלְבְּשִׁי לְבוּשׁ הֲרוּגִים מְטֹעֲנֵי חֶרֶב
לְבוּשׁ אַלְמְנוּת חַיּוּת

לָמָּה קָדְרוּ פָּנֶיךָ לְבָנוֹן הַשַּׁחַר לֹא עוֹלֶה נֶאֱחָז
בַּעֲרָפֶל מוֹרִיד וִילוֹן עַל זִכָּרוֹן, הֶבְזֵק אֶפִּיקוֹרְסִי.
יוֹסִי.
בְּגִ׳יפּ סִי יוּר יוֹשֵׁב רַגְלַיִם אֲרֻכּוֹת גְּמִישׁוֹת כְּנוּסוֹת אֶל
גּוּף צְבָיִי שֶׁל יֶלֶד טוֹב אַשְׁדּוֹד.
עוֹשֶׂה בְּדִיקַת קֶשֶׁר עִם אֱלֹהִים.
אֱלֹהִים שׁוֹמֵעַ, עֲבֹר.
אַחֲרֵי הַהַבְדָּלָה מֵכִין לִי נֵס. נֵס רוֹבָאִית.
אֵיזֶה נֵס! אֵילוּ נִסִּים?
יוֹסִי.

כָּל הַלַּיְלָה בָּעֲרָה הָאֵשׁ וַתֹּאכַל אֶת אַרְזֵי הַלְּבָנוֹן
אֶת דָּנוּךְ זֶהֱתָה לְפִי הַשְּׁנַיִם הַלְּבָנוֹת שֶׁבַּחִיּוּךְ

an embryo grows stabs
so you'll remember!

Open Lebanon your doors and all my winged
visionary soldiers will come
and they will be planted in you like cedars.
Like Yoav like
Nadav.

His look is like that of Lebanon and who has betrothed a wife and
has not taken her
with him in a tongue of flame wants to shout with me
from Lebanon my bride with me
from Lebanon come
clothed with the slain, those pierced by the sword,
the garments of living widowhood

why has your face darkened Lebanon the dawn does not rise caught
in the fog lowering a curtain on memory, a heretic flash.
Yossi.
Sitting in a patrol jeep long flexible legs gathered to
the deer-like body of a good Ashdod boy.
Doing a radio check with God.
God come in, over.
After *havdalah* he makes me coffee. Infantry instant.
The difference an instant makes?!
Yossi.

All night the fire burned consuming the cedars of Lebanon
identifying Danoch by the white teeth of his smile

הֶחְפִּיר לְבָנוֹן קָמַל הָפַךְ חָרוּךְ
כְּשֶׁזֶּרַע נִטְמַן בְּאָבִיו בְּחִבּוּק הַנְּפָשׁוֹת וְאֵל יִשְׁמְרָן
    עֵת לָקְחוּ שַׁלְהָבוֹת בְּמֹשֶׁה וְעֶרָן

כָּל אֶחָד יֵשׁ לוֹ אֶת הַלְּבָנוֹן שֶׁלּוֹ
    לֵב בּוֹעֵר וְאֵינֶנּוּ אֻכָּל
פַּעַם אַחַת חָזַרְתִּי לְשָׁם:
לִלְבָנוֹן בְּשִׁרְיוֹן כְּמוֹ בֶּן רְאֵמִים
    וּמָצָאתִי.
בַּלְּבְנֶה נֶאֶחְזָה קֶרֶן שֶׁל אַיִל. הָאַיִל בָּרַח
    (כְּמוֹ הָרֶגֶל שֶׁל אִיתָמָר שֶׁנּוֹתְרָה בַּסְּבַךְ)
הִיא מוּלִי בַּסָּלוֹן, מֵעַל הַסְּפָרִים
    שׁוֹמֶרֶת שֶׁלֹּא אוֹרִיד מָסָךְ.
אוֹ פַּעַם אַחֵר, מוּל חֶרְמוֹן הַסּוּרִי
    אֲנִי תְּפִלִּין בְּמִקְדָּשׁ יְוָנִי מֻצָּב חוֹדֵר
    אֶת הַשָּׁמַיִם

אֵיפֹה אַתְּ, אִמָּא
עֲלִי הַלְּבָנוֹן וְצַעֲקִי

וְהַהוֹלְכִים אֵינָם מְנִיחִים
אֲנִי הוֹלֵךְ אוֹתָם
    בְּעַל־כָּרְחִי

כָּל אֶחָד יֵשׁ לוֹ אֶת הַלְּבָנוֹן שֶׁלּוֹ
    חַיָּל יָפֶה הָרוּג נִשָּׂא עַל הַכְּתֵפַיִם
וְכָל נַעֲרוֹתָיו מְלַחֲשׁוֹת בָּאֹזֶן אֶת שְׁמוֹתָיו וְהוּא עָלַי וְהוּא
    אִתִּי מִלְּבָנוֹן

ד באייר התש"ס

Lebanon became gutted withered charred
        when a seed was buried in his father in the embrace of souls
and may the Lord guard them
        when flames flared up in Moshe and Eran

every one has his own Lebanon
        a burning heart that is not consumed
once I returned there:
to Lebanon in a tank like a young wild ox
        and I found.
In the birch tree a ram's horn was held. The ram fled
        (like the leg of Itamar which remained in the thicket)
she is opposite me in the living room, above the books
        she guards against my lowering of a curtain.
Or on another occasion, opposite the Syrian Hermon
        I am *tefillin* in a Greek temple a military post penetrating
the heavens

where are you, mother
go up to Lebanon and shout

And those who are going will not let go
        I go with them
                against my will

every one has his own Lebanon
        a handsome dead soldier carried on my shoulders
and all his girls whisper his names and he is upon me and he
        is with me from Lebanon

4th of Iyar, 5760

*

וּבַלֵּילוֹת
אֲנִי מַטְמִין שִׁירִים בַּמְּקוֹמוֹת הַכְּמוּסִים שֶׁבְּגוּפֵךְ
(כְּמוֹ פִּתְקָאוֹת בַּכֹּתֶל)
רוּחַ לוֹטֶפֶת אוֹתָנוּ מְרַפָּה אֵיבָרִים יְגֵעִים
עָמָל וְהֵרָיוֹן.
עוֹד מְעַט בֹּקֶר
הַיְלָדִים יָבוֹאוּ מִתַּחַת לַשְּׂמִיכָה
יִמְצְאוּ אֶת הַשִּׁירִים

*

And at night
I hide poems in the secret parts of your body
        (like notes in the Wall)
a breeze caresses us healing limbs weary
        from labor and pregnancy.
Soon it will be morning
        the children will come in under the covers
        and find the poems

בָּאוּלְטְרָסָאוּנְד

וְכָל הָעָם רוֹאִים אֶת הַקּוֹלוֹת
הִנֵּה, גַּם אֲנַחְנוּ:
לֵב קָטָן רוֹקֵד בְּאָדֹם וְכָחֹל
מַחֲרֹזֶת פְּנִינִים הַשִּׁדְרָה
(אוֹ קַרְנֵי־הַשֶּׁמֶשׁ)
חָמֵשׁ אֶצְבָּעוֹת מְחַפְּשׂוֹת
וְעוֹד חָמֵשׁ
אֵיבַר הַמִּין נֶחְבָּא
(וּמִמֵּילָא לֹא רָצִינוּ לָדַעַת)
מַשֶּׁהוּ רוֹעֵד בָּנוּ מִבִּפְנִים
רוֹצֶה וְלֹא יָכוֹל לָגַעַת

Ultrasound

"And all the people saw the sounds"
        look, we do too: a tiny heart dancing in red and blue
        the spine a pearl necklace
        (or sun rays)
        five fingers searching
        and five more
the sex organ is hidden
        (in any case we didn't want to know)
something is trembling inside us
        wanting but unable to touch

הָלְכָה לָנוּ לְאִבּוּד

בַּבֹּקֶר כְּשֶׁקַּמְנוּ, תֹּפֶת בָּאָזְנַיִם
גִּלִּינוּ שֶׁהָלְכָה לָנוּ הָאָרֶץ לְאִבּוּד.
חִפַּשְׂנוּ עַל הַמֵּצַח, בֵּין הַסְּדִינִים
בְּשֻׁלְחַן הַכְּתִיבָה הַשּׁוֹתֵק. סִימָנִים
נִשְׁכְּחוּ מֵעִמָּנוּ. וְלֹא יָדַעְנוּ עַל מָה
אָבְדָה הָאָרֶץ.
גִּלְגַּלְנוּ הָאַשְׁמָה לְפֶתַח קַדְמוֹן.
כְּאִשָּׁה מְעֻבָּרָה הָיִינוּ, אִשָּׁה
מְעֻבָּרָה חֲבוּשָׁה בְּבֵית הָאֲסוּרִים.
מַה הִיא רוֹאָה?
הַטִּיחַ נִקְלָף בְּסָגֹל חָזָק, כְּמוֹ הַזִּכָּרוֹן.
הַזִּכָּרוֹן מַרְעִיד כְּמוֹ כְּרֵסָהּ שֶׁבֵּין שִׁנֶּיהָ,
בּוֹעֵט כְּעֻבָּר מְנַסֶּה הַזִּכָּרוֹן.
מֵת הַזִּכָּרוֹן.

The Land Lost its Way

When we arose in the morning, an inferno in our ears
we discovered that the land had gone away.
We searched for it on foreheads, between the bed sheets,
on the silent writing desk. The signs
were forgotten. And we knew not why
the land had gone.
We put the blame on an ancient opening.
We were like a pregnant woman, a pregnant
woman locked in a prison.
What does she see?
The plaster peeling in deep purple, like the memory.
The memory trembles in her belly.
Kicking like a fetus the memory tries.
The memory dies.

תְּפִלָּה לַנֶּהָג בִּכְבִישׁ הַמִּנְהָרוֹת

יְהִי רָצוֹן מִלְּפָנֶיךָ
מֶלֶךְ שׁוֹמֵעַ אֶל אֶבְיוֹנִים
הַשּׁוֹמֵר עַל כָּל פְּתָחִים וְחֶבְיוֹנִים
שֶׁתַּצִּילֵנִי מִכָּל תְּלָאוֹת שֶׁבַּדֶּרֶךְ

שֶׁתּוֹלִיכֵנִי לְשָׁלוֹם
וְתַצְעִידֵנִי לְשָׁלוֹם
וְתִשְׁמְרֵנִי מִכָּל מִינֵי הָאֲבָנִים
הָאוֹרְבִים הַמַּשְׁלִיכִים הַיּוֹרִים מִסְתַּנְּנִים
זוֹמְמִים הַמַּחְסוֹמִים אֵלֶּה שֶׁקְּלָלָה מְסַנְּנִים
וּמִכָּל מַבָּטִים הַשּׁוֹטְמִים הַמִּתְרַגְּשִׁים וּבָאִים
לָעוֹלָם
(וּבִשְׁעַת הַחֲשֵׁכָה יוֹסִיף: וּמִכַּוָּנוֹת הַלַּיְלָה)
וְתַגִּיעֵנִי לִמְחוֹז חֶפְצִי
בַּחַיִּים. וּבְשִׂמְחָה וּבְשָׁלוֹם
וּתְנֵנִי לִהְיוֹת נוֹלָד מִתּוֹךְ הַמִּנְהָרָה אֶל יְרוּשָׁלַיִם
וְתִשְׁמַע תְּפִלָּתָם שֶׁל עוֹבְרֵי דְּרָכִים לְפָנֶיךָ
בְּרַחֲמִים

Prayer for the Driver on the Tunnel Road

May it be thy will
        O King who hears the indigent
Who guards all openings and hidden places
May you save me from all the troubles along the way

        May you accompany me in peace
        May you lead me in peace
        May you guard me from all manner of stones
        ambushers who throw shoot infiltrate
        conspire these barriers that sift a curse
        and from all the hateful looks that come suddenly into the
                world
(and at night add: and from the aims of the night)
        and bring me to my destination
        in life. And in joy and in peace
and allow me to be born out of this tunnel into Jerusalem
and may the prayers of the wayfarers be heard before you
        with mercy

מִשִּׁירֵי הַכְּפָר שֶׁבָּהָר [ב]

א.
קִרְקוּר הוֹמֶה שֶׁמִּן הַלּוּלִים
מְטַשְׁטֵשׁ נְהִימוֹת שְׁכִינָה
כְּיוֹנָה בֶּחֳרָבוֹת הַצְּפוֹנִיּוֹת
כְּשֶׁגּוֹבְרִים הַתַּרְנְגוֹלִים
אֲנִי יוֹדֵעַ
כִּי בָּא גוֹאֵל

ב.
הוּא בָּא וְהוֹלֵךְ
נִגְלֶה וְנִכְסֶה בֵּין הַטֶּרָסוֹת
שֶׁבָּנוּ הַדּוֹרוֹת שֶׁהִזְרִיעוּ אוֹתָנוּ
עַל הַגְּבָעוֹת הָאֵלֶּה.
אַתְּ זוֹכֶרֶת
בַּיּוֹם הָרִאשׁוֹן אַחֲרֵי הַגֶּשֶׁם
כְּשֶׁהָלַכְנוּ לְלַקֵּט פִּטְרִיּוֹת
לַעֲקֹב אַחַר הַצְּבָאִים
יָדַעְתִּי שֶׁאָנוּ עוֹקְבִים אַף
אַחֲרָיו.
וְכָל כָּךְ רָצִיתִי לְהַגִּיעַ עָדָם
לִתְפֹּס זְנָבָם הָאָצִיל,
לִרְכֹּב עַל גַּבָּם.
אַחֲרָיו

From Poems of the Mountain Village [b]

a.
A noisy crowing from the chicken coops
blurs the dove-like cooing of the Shekhina
in the northern ruins
when the roosters overcome
I know
the redeemer is coming

b.
He comes and goes
revealed and concealed among the terraces
built by the generations who bred us
on these hills.
You remember
on the first day after the rain
when we went to pick mushrooms
to follow the deer
I knew that we were following
him as well.
How I wanted to reach them
to take hold of their noble tails,
to ride on their backs.
After him

ג.

לִפְעָמִים אֲנִי רוֹאֶה אוֹתוֹ
עָנִי מְחַטֵּט בְּפִצְעָיו
כְּמוֹ הַפּוֹעֵל הָעַרְבִי שֶׁבָּנָה לָנוּ
אֶת הַבַּיִת

ד.

שׁוּב אֲנִי מִתְפַּלֵּל אֶל
הַיֹּפִי הַמִּקְרִי הַזֶּה
שֶׁעַל הַוִּיטְרָאז' מֵעַל אֲרוֹן־הַקֹּדֶשׁ.
אֵיךְ נֶאֶסְפוּ שָׁמָּה כָּל
הָאֲבָנִים הָאֵלֶּה לְעֵדֶר אֶחָד
נִתְמָכִים
כְּמוֹ שְׁלַל אֲבוֹתֵיכֶם, גַּם הֵם
נֹאחֲזוּ בִּשְׁלֹשָׁה סְלָעִים פִּרְאִיִּים

ה.

בְּמַטָּעֵי הַתַּפּוּחִים הָיִיתִי מִסְתַּתֵּר
מִפְּנֵי צְלִיפוֹת מְחֻדָּדוֹת שֶׁל גֶּשֶׁם.
פַּעַם
נִסְתָּרִים הָיוּ מִפְּנֵי קְלִיעֵי עוֹפֶרֶת
פְּלָחֵי מַרְגֵּמָה,
הָיוּ מִתְפַּלְּלִים אֶל הַגֶּשֶׁם הַזֶּה.
כָּאן, תַּחַת הַתַּפּוּחַ, אַהֲבָה גְּדוֹלָה
עוֹרַרְתִּיךְ

c.
Sometimes I see him
a pauper scratching at his sores
like the Arab worker who built
our house

d.
Once again I pray to
this coincidental beauty
on the stained glass above the holy ark.
How did all these stones gather there
to a flock
supported
like the abundance of your fathers, they too
held tightly to three wild rocks

e.
In the apple orchards I would take cover
from the sharp lashings of rain.
Once
taking cover from lead bullets,
mortar fragments,
they prayed for this rain.
Here, under the apple tree, great love,
I awakened you

מַסַּע אָבִיב בְּאֶרֶץ יִשְׂרָאֵל, תשס"ב

בֵּינְתַיִם עוֹד אָבִיב פֹּה בְּאֶרֶץ הַקֹּדֶשׁ
וְרֵיחַ שָׂדֶה מְשַׁכֵּר
יֵשׁ לִבְנֶה מְלַבְלֵב בַּצָּפוֹן וּפְלָגִים מִן
לְבָנוֹן וַהֲמוֹן חַרְדָּלִים מַכִּים בִּנְחִירַיִם
רַק תָּבוֹא וְתִשְׁכַּב כָּאן עַתָּה, בֵּינוֹתֵינוּ
לִמְעַט מְנוּחָה נְכוֹנָה

וּבַלֵּב סְתָו

מִדְרוֹנוֹת רוֹנְנִים בְּאָדֹם וְצָהֹב
אֲפִלּוּ צִפֳּרִים עָפוֹת בַּעֲצִימַת עֵינַיִם
(שֶׁלֹּא לִכְאֹב)
גִּרְגּוּרֵי בְּהֵמוֹת מְסַפְּרִים שֶׁעוֹד יִהְיֶה טוֹב
הָאָרֶץ כֻּלָּהּ זְעוּקָה לֶאֱהֹב

וּבַלֵּב רוּחַ רָעָה, וּסְתָו

הַשְּׁקֵדִיּוֹת כְּמוֹ כַּלּוֹת נֶעֱלָסוֹת בְּהָרֵי יְרוּשָׁלַיִם
וְשַׁחְרוּרִים מַזְכִּירִים צְחוֹק הַיְלָדִים
(שֶׁהָיָה פַּעַם בַּחוּצוֹת)
כְּמוֹ דִּנְדּוּן פַּעֲמוֹנִים
כְּמוֹ פִּכְפּוּךְ הַמַּיִם

וּבַלֵּב צֵל שָׁחוֹר מִתְגַּנֵּב, נִרְאֶה שֶׁסְּתָו

A Spring Journey in the Land of Israel, 5762

In the meantime it is still spring here in the holy land
and the fragrance of a field intoxicates
there is a birch blooming in the north and streams from
Lebanon and myriad mustard plants strike the nostrils
just come and lie down here now, among us
for a brief rest

but in the heart it is autumn

slopes rejoice in yellow and rose
even birds fly with their eyes closed
(preventing pain)
the grunting of animals shows
that good times will come again
the entire land is crying for love

but in the heart is a wicked wind, and autumn

the almond trees are like merry brides in the Jerusalem hills
and blackbirds remind us of the laughter of children
(which was once in the streets)
like the peal of bells
like the trickle of water

but into the heart a black shadow steals, it seems that it's
autumn

כָּאן בַּמַּטָּעִים בְּעֶצְיוֹן, הַכֹּל נִמְלָא תִּקְוָה
בִּפְרִיחַת הַגְּדְגְּדָן
בִּקְצוֹת עַנְפֵי הַתְּאֵנָה כְּבָר מַפְצִיעוֹת
יָדַיִם קְטַנְטַנּוֹת, בּוֹקְשׁוֹת, מִתְחַנְּנוֹת

וְיֵשׁ אֲוִיר וְיֵשׁ שָׁמַיִם וְיֵשׁ אוֹר

וּבַלֵּב עָלִים נוֹשְׁרִים, זֶה סְתָו

הַנִּצָּנִים נִרְאוּ בָּאָרֶץ, עֵת הַזָּמִיר הִגִּיעַ וְקוֹל
הַתּוֹר נִשְׁמַע אָרֹךְ וּמְכַזֵּב

וְאֵיךְ נֵצֵא הַשָּׂדֶה נַשְׁכִּימָה לַכְּרָמִים

וּבַלֵּב סְתָו

here in the orchards of Etzion all is filled with hope
with the blossoming of the cherry trees
at the ends of the fig branches little hands are
already breaking out, seeking, pleading

and there is air and there is sky and there is light

    but in the heart leaves are falling, it is autumn

the flowers appear on the earth, the time of the singing of birds is come
    and the turtledove sounds long and deceiving

Oh how will we go out to the fields, rise early for the vineyards

    when autumn is in the heart

מִשְׁכֵינִי אַחֲרַיִךְ

שלושה הבהובי אהבה

*

אֵלִי, שֶׁלֹּא יִגָּמֵר לְעוֹלָם
הַיָּרֹק הַזֶּה שֶׁבְּעֵינַיִךְ
דִּנְדּוּן צְחוֹק הַיְלָדִים וְגַם
לְטוּף רָאשֵׁיכֶם בַּלַּיְלָה כְּשֶׁאֲנִי מַנִּיחַ לִפְנֵיכֶם
בִּרְכַּת כֹּהֵן לָבָן בַּחֲשֵׁכָה

*

אִם יֵשׁ הֵיכָל שֶׁאֵינוֹ
נִפְתָּח
אֶלָּא בְּנִגּוּן
הַתִּירִי לִי, וּבַחֲלִילִי
(הַדַּק, הַמְנֻקָּב)
שֶׁיָּדַע רִגְעֵי עֶצֶבֶת
נֵדַע שִׂמְחָה

*

מִשְׁכֵינִי אַחֲרַיִךְ – וְאָרוּצָה
אֶל אֲגַס גּוּפֵךְ
אֶל חֶבְיוֹנוֹתַיִךְ

מִשְׁכֵינִי וְאָרוּצָה
מִשְׁכֵינִי וְאָרוּצָה

Draw Me After You

Three flickerings of love

*

my Lord, may it never end:
the green that is in your eyes
the peal of the children's laughter and also
the caressing of their heads at night when I set before them
        a white priest's blessing in the dark

*

if there is a temple
which opens
only with a melody
open for me, and with my flute
(thin, pierced)
which knew moments of sadness
we will know joy

*

draw me after you – and I shall run
        to the pear of your body
        to your hiding places

draw me and I shall run
draw me and I shall run

פֶּסַח פָּלַשְׂתִּינִי

עַד מָתַי לֹא תִּפְסַח הָרָעָה עַל בָּתֵּינוּ
רְאֵה, כְּבָר מָשַׁחְנוּ הַפֶּתַח בְּדָם
צְנוּפִים אִישׁ לְבֵית־אָבוֹת, זָעַקְנוּ
בְּשֶׁקֶט־אָדָם

רְאֵה אַרְבַּע כּוֹסוֹתֵינוּ מָלְאוּ
יַיִן סָמוּק וְרָתוּחַ
לְשׁוֹנוֹתֵינוּ לְשֶׁל אֵשׁ הָיוּ
כְּשֶׂה טָבוּחַ

אִם גַּם רֹאשֵׁנוּ שַׁח – וְעֶצֶב סוֹבְבָנוּ
הָבָה וְנִתְלַקַּח:
יְהוּדִים דְּשֵׁנִים בּוֹעֲרִים הֵיטֵב
וּמַה יִּוָּתֵר מִמֶּנּוּ עַד בֹּקֶר?

כִּסֵּא רֵיק. בַּחֲצַר כְּנֵסִיַּת הַמָּשִׁיחַ הַמֵּת
מְחַכֶּה לְרָאִיס שֶׁיֵּצֵא לַחָפְשִׁי
שֶׁיָּבוֹא וְיִגְאַל

אֲנִי רוֹאֶה אוֹתוֹ כְּמוֹ אָז, יִשְׁמַעְאֵל מְצַחֵק
בַּלַּיְלָה הַזֶּה
אֵין בַּיִת בְּאֶרֶץ הַקֹּדֶשׁ אֲשֶׁר אֵין שָׁם

עַכְשָׁו הוּא מוֹסִיף עוֹד סְאָה
לִקְעָרַת הַדָּמִים

A Palestinian Passover

Until when will the evil not pass over our homes
look, we have already anointed the entrance with blood
each man enwrapped in his ancestral home, we cried out
        in human silence

look, our four cups are filled
with flushed boiling wine
our tongues have become tongues of fire
        like a slaughtered lamb

if our head is also bowed – and sadness surrounds us
let us flare up:
lush Jews burn well
and what will remain of us until the morning?

An empty chair. In the courtyard of the church of the dead messiah
waits for the *Rais* to be released
        to come and redeem

I see him as before, Ishmael mocking
        on that night
there is no house in the holy land where there is not

now he adds another measure
        to the bowl of blood

עוֹד מְעַט יֵאָפֶה לֶחֶם הָעֹנִי הַגָּדוֹל
שֶׁל שְׁנֵי הָעַמִּים

שיר זה נדפס בעיתון "מקור ראשון", בפתח מוסף ליל-
הסדר התשס"ב, הלילה בו אירע הטבח במלון פארק
בנתניה. פחות מארבעים ושמונה שעות לאחר מכן כבר
הייתי על סיפון הטנק, מתכונן למערכה על שכם

soon will be baked the bread of great affliction
of both nations

This poem appeared in the holiday supplement of the newspaper "Makor Rishon" which came out on Passover Eve 2002. On that night the horrendous Seder night terrorist attack at the Park Hotel in Netanya took place. Less than 48 hours later I was on a tank preparing for battle in Nablus.

שירים ליוצא למלחמה

The Poet Goes to War

*

בַּשֵּׁנִי בְּשַׁבָּת בַּחֹדֶשׁ הַשְּׁלִישִׁי בְּשִׁשָּׁה בַּחֹדֶשׁ תָּ"ו שִׁי"ן
סָמֶ"ךְ אָלֶ"ף
נִפְתְּחוּ הַשָּׁמַיִם
וָאֶרְאֶה מַרְאוֹת אֱלֹהִים

חָשׂוּף בַּצָּרִיחַ
הַטַּנְק שֶׁלִּי בּוֹעֵר מֵעַל גֶ'נִין הָעִיר
מַדְהִיר אוֹתִי בְּלֶהָבוֹת
וְכָל הָרַקָּפוֹת כּוֹמְסוֹת אֱלֵי סַלְעָן
יָד שְׁחוֹרָה גְּדוֹלָה עָקְרָה בְּמִגְדְּלֵי הַמִּסְגָּדִים
רוֹצָה לִדְקֹר לִבִּי בְּסַהַר מְעֻקָּל
בַּסַּלְצָרִיחַ אִשָּׁה וִילָדִים רַכִּים וּמִסָּבִיב סְגַלְגַּל
וְאַרְגָּמָן. דָּבָר עוֹד לֹא נָפַל

אִם יַד עָנָן תָּבוֹא וְלָקְחָה עַכְשָׁו אֶל
יַעַר הַשְּׁקֵדִים שֶׁלֹּא רָחוֹק מִכָּאן

הָיִינוּ עוֹרְכִים אֲהָבוֹת בֵּין כָּל עִיֵּי הֶחֳרָבוֹת

*

on the second day of the week on the sixth day of the third month
in the year 5 7 6 1
the sky opened
and I saw visions of God

exposed in the turret
my burning tank above the city of Jenin
carries me galloping in flames
and all the cyclamens withdraw to their rock
a large detached black hand in the towers of the mosques
wants to stab my heart with a curved crescent
in the turret-basket is a woman and young children and surrounding
them
lavender and purple. Nothing has transpired yet

should the hand of a cloud come and take now to
the almond forest not far from here

we would arrange assignations among all the ruins

שְׁכֶם שַׁבְנוּ אֵלַיִךְ

שַׁבְנוּ אֵלַיִךְ לְבָה מְדַמֶּמֶת
עִיר מוּעֶדֶת פֻּרְעָנוּת
בָּךְ חָנָה אַבְרָם לַחֲנִיַּת הַלַּיְלָה הָרִאשׁוֹן בֶּהָרִים
עִיר בְּמִסְתָּרִים בָּךְ
אִישׁ מְחַפֵּשׂ אַחִים בְּדֶרֶךְ רְחוֹקָה
בָּךְ נִפְלְגָה הַמַּמְלָכָה
בָּךְ הִתְפַּלַּלְתִּי פַּעַם הַמִּנְחָה
בֵּין מְנַשֶּׁה לְבֵין אֶפְרַיִם

הוֹ עִיר אֲרֻכָּה וַעֲמֻקָּה
בֵּין גְּרִיזִים לְעֵיבָל אֲנִי
עֹז וְאַהֲבָה
(שֶׁהַקְּלָלָה לֹא לְרֹאשֵׁנוּ תִּפֹּל)
הוֹ יוֹסֵף צַדִּיקָא
לוּ לֹא עוֹד נִדַּמֵּם לַמָּוֶת

Nablus, We have Returned to You

We have returned to you bleeding core
calamity prone city
in you Abraham camped on his first night in the mountains
a city with hiding places
a man searches for brothers on a distant road
in you the kingdom was divided
in you I once prayed the afternoon prayer
between Menashe and Ephraim

O city long and deep
between Gerizim and Ebal am I
strength and love
(may the curse not fall upon our heads)
O *Yuseph Zadika*
if only we will bleed to death no more

וּבִשְׁעַת הַמִּלְחָמָה

הצעה לנוסח חדש

רמב"ם, הלכות מלכים ומלחמותיהם

פרק שביעי הלכה ט"ו

וּמֵאַחַר שֶׁיִּכָּנֵס בְּקִשְׁרֵי הַמִּלְחָמָה
יִשָּׁעֵן עַל מִקְוֵה יִשְׂרָאֵל וּמוֹשִׁיעוֹ
בְּעֵת צָרָה (כֵּן יְהִי עִמָּנוּ)

וְיֵדַע שֶׁעַל יִחוּד הַשֵּׁם הוּא עוֹשֶׂה מִלְחָמָה וְיָשִׂים
נַפְשׁוֹ בְּכַפּוֹ (וְאַף יִנְצְרֶנָּה)
וְלֹא יִירָא וְלֹא יִפְחַד
וְיַחְשֹׁב בְּאִשְׁתּוֹ וּבְבָנָיו וּבְבִתּוֹ
(הָרַחֲמָן הוּא יְבָרֵךְ אוֹתִי וְאֶת אֶפְרָת
וְאֶת אֲחִיָּה וְאֶת אוֹרִיָּה וְאֶת שָׁקֵד וְאֶת מִרְיָם)
שֶׁגַּם לְמַעֲנָם הוּא עוֹשֶׂה חַיִל
וּכְשֶׁיָּשׁוּב בְּשָׁלוֹם אֶל חֵיק הַחִבּוּק הַגָּדוֹל
יָשׁוּב

And in Time of War

a suggestion for a new version of Maimonides,
Laws of Kings and Their Wars,
Chapter 7, law 15

Once, however, he has joined the ranks,
he should put his reliance upon Him who is the hope of Israel, their savior
in time of trouble (so may it be with us)

He should know that he is fighting for the oneness of God, and shall put
his life in his hands (and guard it as well)
and neither fear nor be affrighted.
And he shall think of his wife and his sons and his daughter
(may the merciful One bless me and Efrat
and Achia and Oria and Shaked and Miriam)
for his heroism is for them too
and when he returns in peace, to the heart of the great embrace
shall he return

בִּשְׁכֶם רָאִיתִי

בִּשְׁכֶם רָאִיתִי פָּנֶיהָ הַיָּפוֹת שֶׁל הַמִּלְחָמָה
כְּפָנַיִךְ הַחֲרֵדוֹת בַּבַּיִת
עֶרֶב שַׁבָּת הָיָה כְּשֶׁנִּקְרֵאתִי
אֵיךְ בֵּרַכְנוּ הַיְלָדִים בִּרְעָדָה

בִּשְׁכֶם רָאִיתִי פָּנֶיהָ הַיָּפוֹת שֶׁל הַמִּלְחָמָה
כִּפְנֵי לְבָנָה בִּמְלוֹאָהּ
עִם שְׁדֵרַת מַרְכְּבוֹת הַפְּלָדָה
בְּעֵת הַנֶּשֶׁף מוּאָרָה

בִּשְׁכֶם רָאִיתִי פָּנֶיהָ הַיָּפוֹת שֶׁל הַמִּלְחָמָה
כִּפְנֵי הַיַּלְדָּה הַפָּלַשְׂתִּינִית
נִצְמֶדֶת אֶל יֶרֶךְ אָבִיהָ
בְּפֶתַח בֵּיתָהּ הַנָּצוּר מִפָּנַי

בִּשְׁכֶם רָאִיתִי פָּנֶיהָ הַיָּפוֹת שֶׁל הַמִּלְחָמָה
כִּפְנֵי לוֹחֲמִים מִזְדַּהֲרִים
בְּטֶרֶם קְרָב
וַעֲדַיִן אֵינֶנִּי יָכוֹל לָתֵת תֹּאַר
לְמַה שֶּׁרָאִיתִי בִּשְׁכֶם

In Nablus I Saw

In Nablus I saw the pretty face of war
like your anxious face at home
on Sabbath Eve I was called up
how we blessed the children fearfully

In Nablus I saw the pretty face of war
like the face of the full moon
with a row of steel chariots
lit up at night time

In Nablus I saw the pretty face of war
like the face of the Palestinian girl
clinging to the leg of her father
at the entrance to her house which is besieged before me

In Nablus I saw the pretty face of war
like the glowing faces of fighters
prior to battle
and I still cannot describe
what I saw in Nablus

מִי שֶׁחָלַם

מִי שֶׁחָלַם אֶל חֵיקֵךְ
בְּטֶרֶם שֶׁלָּחַם
וְטָעַם דְּבְשֵׁךְ מִן הַמִּדְבָּר
מִמְּשֻׁלַּשׁ   הַכָּחֹל וְהֶעָמֹק שֶׁל יָם
הַמֶּלַח

שֶׁאֶת שִׁיר־הַשִּׁירִים מֵרֵר בִּבְכִי־עֶרְגוֹנוֹת
שֶׁהָפַךְ יוֹנַת־אֵלֶם
הָאֶלֶף לְךָ שְׁלֹמֹה
וְלִי הָאַחַת רְחוֹקָה רְחוֹקָה הָיְתָה

מִי שֶׁנִּפְשְׁקוּ אֶצְבְּעוֹתָיו בִּשְׁחוֹר הַלַּיִל
לְדָרוֹם וּלְמִזְרָח

נָמַסּוּ אֵיבָרָיו וּלְבָבוֹ בְּאַהֲבוֹ
שֶׁעֲטַפְתִּינִי כְּטַלִּית בְּעֵת שַׁחֲרִית
וְרֶטֶט הֶבְלֵךְ בִּמְחוֹשֵׁי עָרְפִּי
כִּי גְּאַלְתִּינִי

He Who Dreamed

Who dreamed to your breast
before he fought
and tasted your honey from the desert
from the deep blue   triangle of the
                    Dead Sea

Who embittered the Song of Songs with a yearning-cry
        which turned into a silent dove
O Solomon must have a thousand
and I only one far far away

Whose fingers spread wide in the black of night
        to the south and to the east

        His limbs and his heart melted with his love
        which enwrapped me like a prayer shawl at morning
        and your quivering breath at the antennae of my nape
        for you redeemed me

עֲקוּדָה

(מדרש לבראשית כ"ב, א–י"ד)

וַיְהִי אַחַר הַדְּבָרִים הָאֵלֶּה וְהָאֱלֹהִים נִסָּה אֶת־אַבְרָהָם. וַיֹּאמֶר אֵלָיו אַבְרָהָם וַיֹּאמֶר הִנֵּנִי: וַיֹּאמֶר קַח־נָא אֶת־בִּנְךָ אֶת־יְחִידְךָ אֲשֶׁר־אָהַבְתָּ אֶת־יִצְחָק וְלֶךְ־לְךָ אֶל־אֶרֶץ הַמֹּרִיָּה וְהַעֲלֵהוּ שָׁם לְעֹלָה עַל אַחַד הֶהָרִים אֲשֶׁר אֹמַר אֵלֶיךָ:

וְשׁוּב קָרְאוּ לוֹ הָרוּחוֹת.\
מְעַט יָשַׁב. כִּמְעַט חָלַץ אֶת סַנְדָּלָיו\
כְּאִלּוּ מִשָּׁמַיִם\
רוּחַ גְּדוֹלָה מַכָּה בַּיְרִיעוֹת. חוֹצָה זְקָנוֹ הָרַךְ\
מִצְחוֹ נִבְקָע לִשְׁנַיִם\
אֲנִי וְהוּא עַכְשָׁו כִּשְׁנֵי זָרִים. כַּעֲרִירִים.\
טוֹב שֶׁיֵּשׁ יִצְחָק בָּאֹהֶל

וַיַּשְׁכֵּם אַבְרָהָם בַּבֹּקֶר וַיַּחֲבֹשׁ אֶת־חֲמֹרוֹ וַיִּקַּח אֶת־שְׁנֵי נְעָרָיו אִתּוֹ וְאֵת יִצְחָק בְּנוֹ וַיְבַקַּע עֲצֵי עֹלָה וַיָּקָם וַיֵּלֶךְ אֶל־הַמָּקוֹם אֲשֶׁר־אָמַר־לוֹ הָאֱלֹהִים:

בַּבֹּקֶר הָרִאשׁוֹן\
לֹא יוֹדַעַת מַה קָּרָה אוֹתִי\
(שֶׁאֵינִי מִמְּאַחֲרֵי קוּם)\
הַמַּחְצֶלֶת הַקְּטַנָּה שֶׁבַּקָּצֶה חַמָּה עוֹדֶנָּה\
שְׁאֵרִיּוֹת שֶׁל רֹק מָתוֹק.\
כְּאִלּוּ מֵרָחוֹק\
תַּרְנְגוֹלוֹת שֶׁבֶּחָצֵר כִּתְמוֹל שִׁלְשׁוֹם\
אֶפְרוֹחַ בְּאִמּוֹ. הָאָב בַּצַּד, כְּמוֹ קוֹרֵא אֵצֶל עַצְמוֹ

Her Sacrifice

(Midrash on Genesis 22, 1–14)

After these things God tested Abraham, and said to him, "Abraham!" And he said, "Here am I." He said, "Take your son, your only son Isaac, whom you love, and go to the land of Mori'ah, and offer him there as a burnt offering upon one of the mountains of which I shall tell you."

And again the winds called to him.
He sat for a while. Almost removed his sandals
as though from heaven
a great wind strikes at the tent cloth. Dividing his soft beard
his forehead split in two
I and he like two strangers now. Like childless people.
How good it is that Isaac is in the tent.

So Abraham rose early in the morning, saddled his ass, and took two of his young men with him, and his son Isaac; and he cut the wood for the burnt offering, and arose and went to the place of which God had told him.

On the first morning
I knew not what was happening to me
(for I am not a late riser)
the little mat in the corner was still warm
remains of sweet saliva.
As though from a distance
chickens in the yard as usual
A chick with its mother. The father is off to the side, as though

בַּלַּיְלָה מִתְכַּרְבֶּלֶת בַּמַּחְצֶלֶת הַקְּטַנָּה שׁוֹמֶרֶת אֶת חֲמוֹ

בַּבֹּקֶר הַשֵּׁנִי חֲמוֹר נוֹעֵר. חֲמוֹר זָקֵן. הָרֶחֶם מִתְרוֹקֵן
רוֹאָה בַּלַּיְלָה אִישׁ עִוֵּר כְּהֵה־רַגְלַיִם מוּבָל בְּיַד עוֹלָל
רוֹצָה צוֹעֶקֶת

בַּיּוֹם הַשְּׁלִישִׁי עָנָן לָבָן עוֹטֵף. אֲנִי כְּמַעְיָן חָרֵב.

בַּיּוֹם הַשְּׁלִישִׁי וַיִּשָּׂא אַבְרָהָם אֶת־עֵינָיו וַיַּרְא אֶת־הַמָּקוֹם מֵרָחֹק: וַיֹּאמֶר אַבְרָהָם אֶל־נְעָרָיו שְׁבוּ־לָכֶם פֹּה עִם־הַחֲמוֹר וַאֲנִי וְהַנַּעַר נֵלְכָה עַד־כֹּה וְנִשְׁתַּחֲוֶה וְנָשׁוּבָה אֲלֵיכֶם:

מֵרָחוֹק נִרְאֶה הָיָה כְּאִלּוּ
לִפְנוֹת בֹּקֶר כְּשֶׁיָּצָא, נָשַׁק מִצְחִי קַלּוֹת
נוּ־בֶּאֱמֶת, תַּעְתּוּעִים שֶׁל בְּלוֹת
מֵרָחוֹק נִרְאֶה הָיָה כְּאִלּוּ
הֵם קְרֵבִים

וַיִּקַּח אַבְרָהָם אֶת־עֲצֵי הָעֹלָה וַיָּשֶׂם עַל־יִצְחָק בְּנוֹ וַיִּקַּח בְּיָדוֹ אֶת־הָאֵשׁ וְאֶת־הַמַּאֲכֶלֶת וַיֵּלְכוּ שְׁנֵיהֶם יַחְדָּו: וַיֹּאמֶר יִצְחָק אֶל־אַבְרָהָם אָבִיו וַיֹּאמֶר אָבִי וַיֹּאמֶר הִנֶּנִּי בְנִי וַיֹּאמֶר הִנֵּה הָאֵשׁ וְהָעֵצִים וְאַיֵּה הַשֶּׂה לְעֹלָה:

בְּקַו רֶכֶס אַחֲרוֹן, רוֹאָה עַכְשָׁו
(כְּמוֹ בַּתֵּיאַטְרוֹן)
שְׁנַיִם עַמּוּדִים שֶׁל אֵשׁ רוֹקְדִים בַּסָּךְ

crowing to himself
at night I curl up on the little mat preserving his warmth

On the second morning a donkey brays. An old donkey. The
womb empties
I see at night a dark-legged blind man led by an infant.
I want to shout

On the third day a white cloud envelops. I am like a dry well.

On the third day Abraham lifted up his eyes and saw the place afar off. Then Abraham said to his young men, "Stay here with the ass; I and the lad will go yonder and worship, and come again to you."

From a distance it seemed as though
when he left at dawn, he kissed my forehead lightly
really now, menopausal delusions
from far it seemed that
they are approaching

And Abraham took the wood of the burnt offering, and laid it on Isaac his son; and he took in his hand the fire and the knife. So they went both of them together. And Isaac said to his father Abraham, "My father!" And he said, "Here am I, my son." He said, "Behold, the fire and the wood; but where is the lamb for a burnt offering?"

On the last ridge, I see now
(as in the theater)
two pillars of fire dancing in

אֶחָד קָטָן
מֵאַחֲרֵיהֶם עָנָן הָרַךְ
כְּמוֹ מָסָךְ מַסְתִּיר מִפְלֶצֶת אוֹ
שָׂטָן.
אֲנִי צוֹעֶקֶת: הִנְנִי בְּנִי בְּנִי
אֲנִי עוֹלָה

וַיֹּאמֶר אַבְרָהָם אֱלֹהִים יִרְאֶה־לּוֹ הַשֶּׂה לְעוֹלָה בְּנִי וַיֵּלְכוּ שְׁנֵיהֶם יַחְדָּו: וַיָּבֹאוּ אֶל־הַמָּקוֹם אֲשֶׁר אָמַר־לוֹ הָאֱלֹהִים וַיִּבֶן שָׁם אַבְרָהָם אֶת־הַמִּזְבֵּחַ וַיַּעֲרֹךְ אֶת־הָעֵצִים וַיַּעֲקֹד אֶת־יִצְחָק בְּנוֹ וַיָּשֶׂם אֹתוֹ עַל־הַמִּזְבֵּחַ מִמַּעַל לָעֵצִים:

נִזְכֶּרֶת אֵיךְ אֶת סַנְדָּלָיו הִשְׁלִיךְ אֶל תּוֹךְ
נָהָר גָּדוֹל, יָחֵף הָלַךְ.
כָּל הַנֶּפֶשׁ שֶׁחָלַמְנוּ בְּחָרָן חָלְצָה אֶת כְּסוּיֶיהָ,
נִשְׁמֶטֶת עֵירֻמָּה.
רוֹאָה אֶת כָּל הַנֶּפֶשׁ שֶׁעָשִׂינוּ עוֹמֶדֶת יְחֵפָה וּרְעוּדָה
אֶל סַף הָהָר. עַכְשָׁו
הַיַּעַר מְבֹעָר. וְהֶעָנָן סָר.

וַיִּשְׁלַח אַבְרָהָם אֶת־יָדוֹ וַיִּקַּח אֶת־הַמַּאֲכֶלֶת לִשְׁחֹט אֶת־בְּנוֹ: וַיִּקְרָא אֵלָיו מַלְאַךְ יי מִן־הַשָּׁמַיִם וַיֹּאמֶר אַבְרָהָם אַבְרָהָם וַיֹּאמֶר הִנֵּנִי:

אַבְרָהָם אַבְרָהָם כַּמָּה רָצִיתִי לִהְיוֹת מְצַחֶקֶת כָּךְ
לִהְיוֹת מְצַעֶקֶת
מַמְשִׁיכָה נוֹפֶלֶת וּכְבָר אֵיבָרַי מִתְפַּזְּרִים נִזְרָעִים בַּחוֹלוֹת
גַּרְגְּרִים קְטַנִּים עֲלֵיהֶם תָּשׁוּבוּ יַחְדָּו

one little procession
behind them a soft cloud
like a curtain covering a monster or
Satan.
I cry out: here I am my son my son
I rise, an offering

Abraham said, "God will provide himself the lamb for a burnt offering, my son." So they went both of them together. When they came to the place of which God had told him, Abraham built an altar there, and laid the wood in order, and bound Isaac his son, and laid him on the altar, upon the wood.

I remember how he threw his sandals into
a great river, wandering barefoot.
All the souls that we dreamed in Haran removed their coverings,
breathing naked.
I see the soul we made standing barefoot and trembling
at the brink of the mountain. Now
the forest is burning. And the cloud moves away.

Then Abraham put forth his hand, and took the knife to slay his son. But the angel of the Lord called to him from heaven, and said, "Abraham, Abraham!" And he said, "Here am I."

Abraham Abraham how I wanted to be playing so
to be screaming
I continue, falling and my limbs are already scattered planted
in the sands
little grains upon them you shall return together

וַיֹּאמֶר אַל־תִּשְׁלַח יָדְךָ אֶל־הַנַּעַר וְאַל־תַּעַשׂ לוֹ מְאוּמָה כִּי עַתָּה יָדַעְתִּי כִּי־יְרֵא אֱלֹהִים אַתָּה וְלֹא־חָשַׂכְתָּ אֶת־בִּנְךָ אֶת־יְחִידְךָ מִמֶּנִּי: וַיִּשָּׂא אַבְרָהָם אֶת־עֵינָיו וַיַּרְא וְהִנֵּה־אַיִל אַחַר נֶאֱחַז בַּסְּבַךְ בְּקַרְנָיו וַיֵּלֶךְ אַבְרָהָם וַיִּקַּח אֶת־הָאַיִל וַיַּעֲלֵהוּ לְעֹלָה תַּחַת בְּנוֹ:

נוֹשֵׂאת עֵינַיִם חֲשׁוּכוֹת –
פַּעַם רָאִיתִי אַיִל רַב אוֹנִים, הֲמוֹן גּוֹיִים
אֵיכָה מַגָּעֵךְ חָשַׂכְתָּ, אִישׁ שֶׁלִּי
אָחוּז בַּסְּבַךְ

וַיִּקְרָא אַבְרָהָם שֵׁם־הַמָּקוֹם הַהוּא יי יִרְאֶה אֲשֶׁר יֵאָמֵר הַיּוֹם בְּהַר יי יֵרָאֶה:

וּמַה יֵּאָמֵר וּמִי יֵרָאֶה

לַשָּׁב מִן הֶהָרִים הַיּוֹם

He said, "Do not lay your hand on the lad or do anything to him; for now I know that you fear God, seeing you have not withheld your son, your only son, from me."

And Abraham lifted up his eyes and looked, and behold, behind him was a ram, caught in a thicket by his horns; and Abraham went and took the ram, and offered it up as a burnt offering instead of his son.

I raise dark eyes –
once I saw a most powerful ram, a multitude of nations
how did you withhold your touch, my man
entangled in the thicket

So Abraham called the name of that place The Lord will provide; as it is said to this day, "On the mount of the Lord it shall be seen."

and what will be said and who will appear

to the one who returns from the mountains today

שִׁיר עַל תֵּל וְאַל אָבִיב

הוֹי תֵּל אָבִיב
זוֹנַת שָׁלוֹם מְנַהֶמֶת
פּוֹרֶשֶׂת אֶבְרוֹתֶיהָ, בֶּטֶן נֶחְשֶׂפֶת
שְׁכִינָה מְעֻלֶּפֶת

הוֹי תֵּל אָבִיב עִיר נִדְהֶמֶת
פּוֹעֶרֶת אֵיבָרִים לְבוֹעֲלִים זָרִים
אִי לָךְ מַלְכַּת הַחוֹל
כָּל גִּבְעָה.

הוֹי תֵּל אָבִיב הַכְנִיסִינִי הַכְנִיסִינִי תַּחַת
כְּנָפֵךְ הַנִּשְׁחֶתֶת
אָבוֹא בָּךְ מָזוֹר.

הוֹ זוֹנָתִי בְּסֵתֶר הַמַּדְרֵגָה הַרְאִינִי
בְּגַן הַהַרְפַּתְקָאוֹת שֶׁלָּנוּ חֲפִיסוֹת אֶקְסְטָזִי שְׁבַטְבָּט
וּמַעֲשִׂים שֶׁל סְדוֹם.
לְאָן הָלַךְ אָבִיב

הוֹי תֵּל אָבִיב תֵּל אָבִיב, חוֹל וִיוָן
עִיר שׁוֹקַעַת
אֵי חַסְדֵּךְ וְאֵי נְעוּרַיִךְ
וְאֵי מִדְבָּר שֶׁיָּשׁוּב לְכַסּוֹתֵךְ

מִי יִבְנֶה יִבְנֶה בַּיִת בְּתֵל אָבִיב?
רַק תִּבְחַר:

Poem On Tel and Not Aviv

Alas! Tel Aviv
cooing whore of peace
spreading her wings, belly exposed,
fainting Shekhinah

Alas! Tel Aviv amazed city
opening wide her limbs to foreign fornicators
Woe to you! queen of the sand,
every hill.

Alas! Tel Aviv take me in take me in under
your corrupt wing
I will come into you cured.

Oh! my whore in the covert of the cliff let me see
in our garden of adventures packets of ecstasy horsetail
and acts of Sodom.
Where has Aviv gone

Alas! Tel Aviv, sand and mire
sinking city
where is your grace and where is your youth
and where is a desert to return and cover you

Who will build will build a house in Tel Aviv?
Only choose:

יֵשׁ לָנוּ בַּיִת חַד־קוֹמָתִי, דוּ־מִינִי וְרַב־הוֹרִי
יֵשׁ גַּם רַב־מִינִי, דוּ־קוֹמָתִי וְחַד־הוֹרִי
יֵשׁ דוּ־הוֹרִי, רַב־קוֹמָתִי וְחַד־מִינִי
מִי יִבְנֶה בַּיִת

בְּתֵל אָבִיב, עִיר כּוֹס
מוֹפּוֹלִיטִית עֲצֵבָה מָתַי יָבוֹאוּ בָּךְ גַּלֵּי
הַיָּם יֶהֱמָיוּן יֶהֱמָיוּן
חוֹלוֹת נִכְסָפִים אֵלַיִךְ תֵּל אָבִיב
בְּשֵׁינְקִין פַּעַם הָיְתָה לִי הִתְגַּלּוּת עַכְשָׁו
אֲנִי שָׁבוּי בְּסֶלַע הַר מֵצִיץ
לָךְ
טוֹבֶלֶת רַגְלַיִם מִשְׁתַּזְּפוֹת בִּקְצוֹת הַמַּיִם

אַי תֵּל אָבִיב, עִיר הַזּוֹנָה
קַמְתְּ לִבְרֹחַ יָפוֹ מִלִּפְנֵי הַשֵּׁם
עוֹד מְעַט דָּג גָּדוֹל יָבוֹא וְיִבְלָעֵךְ

גַּלִּים יַכּוּ בַּיָּם עוֹקְרִים חוֹלוֹת וּמְגַדְּלִים
תִּלֵּי־תִלִּים בְּזַעַם
אַסְפַּקְלַרְיַת גְּוָנִים כְּחֳלִים
לָאֱלֹהִים הַנֶּחְמָלִים

אַתְּ בִּמְעֵי הַדָּג תִּגְעִי קַלּוֹת
תְּדַגְדְּגִי בַּבֶּטֶן הָרַכָּה
הוּא יְקִיאֵךְ

בַּת־יָם קְטַנָּה וְעֵירֻמָּה תִּהְיִי עוֹלָה מִן הָאֲדָווֹת
אֲנִי אָרוּץ וַאֲחַבְּקֵךְ

We have a one-storey home, bisexual and multi-parented
we also have multi-sexual, two-storey and single parent
we have bi-parent, multi-storied and uni-sexual
        Who will build a house

In Tel Aviv, sad cont
    inental city waves of the sea
        will enter you sighing sighing
sands are yearning for you Tel Aviv

Once on Sheinken street I had a revelation now
I am bound to a mountain rock peeping at
    you
dipping tanning legs at the edge of the water

O! Tel Aviv, city of the whore
    you rose to flee from the presence of God to Jaffa
soon a giant fish will come and swallow you

Waves splash in the sea uprooting sands and towers
    heap upon heap in anger
blue hues mirroring
    the pitied LORD
.
You in the bowels of the fish will touch lightly
        Tickling in the soft belly
he will vomit you out
Little nude mermaid you shall rise from the ripples
    I will run and hug you

שֶׁלֶג

שֶׁלֶג עַל יְרוּשָׁלַיִם הַמְדַמֶּמֶת
כְּמוֹ לְחַתֵּל פְּצָעֶיהָ
הַכֹּל נָח בְּשַׁלְוָה עַכְשָׁו
מְמַלֵּא סִדְקֵי גַּעְגּוּעִים שֶׁבַּכֹּתֶל
יְלָדִים בִּרְחוֹבוֹתַיִךְ יְרוּשָׁלַיִם
בְּנֵי יִצְחָק וְיִשְׁמָעֵאל
מְצַחֲקִים מִלְחָמוֹת לְבָנוֹת
(וּפְגִיעָתָם רַכָּה)

אֲפִלּוּ הַיּוֹנִים מִזְדָּרְזוֹת הַיּוֹם
מְנַהֲמוֹת כִּי מָצְאוּ עֲקֵבוֹת חֲדָשִׁים
בַּדֶּרֶךְ הָעוֹלָה אֶל שַׁעַר הָרַחֲמִים

Snow

Snow on bleeding Jerusalem
as though bandaging her wounds
all rests in tranquility now
filling the cracks of yearning in the Wall
children in your streets, Jerusalem
the sons of Isaac and Ishmael
are staging white wars
(and their blows are soft)

even the pigeons are hurrying today
cooing because they have found new footprints
on the way leading up to the Gate of Mercy

הִנֵּה בָּא מְשִׁיחֵנוּ

(בעקבות אצ"ג)

הִנֵּה בָּא מְשִׁיחֵנוּ רָכוּב עַל אֲרִי
אִישׁ לֹא יַכִּירֶנּוּ:
כֻּלָּם מְסֻגָּרִים בַּבָּתִּים. בִּרְחוֹבוֹת תֵּל אָבִיב
סוֹעֵר נוֹטֵף מֹר עוֹבֵר
הָאֲרִי וְעָלָיו מְשִׁיחֵנוּ.
אֵם מְעַטֶּפֶת תִּינוֹק, מְהַדֶּקֶת.
הַיּוֹם חַם, בּוֹעֵר כַּתַּנּוּר
רַק הַיָּם רוֹגֵעַ. עִקְבוֹת הַזָּהָב נִצְרָבוֹת

דּוֹהֵר הָאֲרִי וְעָלָיו הַמָּשִׁיחַ עַד יָפוֹ
וּמִשָּׁם מְנַתֵּר בִּשְׁפֵלַת יְהוּדָה דֶּרֶךְ שַׁעַר הַגַּיְא
נִמְלָא מַחֲטֵי אֳרָנִים (גַּם בִּזְקַן הַמָּשִׁיחַ)
מַסּוֹק מִשְׁטַרְתִּי עָג מֵעָלָיו

בָּרַדְיוֹ בִּקְשׁוּ לֹא לָצֵאת
אַרְיֵה וְעָלָיו תִּמְהוֹנִי בָּרְחוּ מִגַּן הַחַיּוֹת
עוֹד מְעַט יִסְתַּיֵּם הַמָּצוֹד.
אֶפְשָׁר לְהַמְשִׁיךְ לִחְיוֹת.

Here Comes Our Messiah

(after Uri Zvi Greenberg)

Here comes our Messiah riding on a lion
no one will recognize him:
all are shut up in their houses. In the streets of Tel Aviv
the lion rages dripping myrrh,
the Messiah upon him.
A mother swathes her infant, tightly.
The day is hot, burning like an oven
only the sea is calm. The footprints of gold are scorched.

The lion with the Messiah upon him gallops to Jaffa
and from there leaps the plains of Judah through Sh'ar Hagai
filling with pine needles (in the beard of the Messiah as well)
a police helicopter circles above

on the radio they asked not to go outside
a lion with a weirdo upon him escaped from the zoo
the pursuit will soon end.
You can go on living.

עוֹד תִּרְאֶה

עוֹד תִּרְאֶה, בַּשָּׁנָה הַבָּאָה
מֵעַל לָהָר
עָנָן יַעֲלֶה אֲדַמְדַּם
וּפָנָיו פְּנֵי אֲרִי
תַּ"ק עַל תַּ"ק, בֵּין אַשְׁמוּרָה לְאַשְׁמוּרָה
יִרְעֲדוּ בַּשְּׁאָגָה הַנִּכְמָרָה

עוֹד תִּרְאֶה, בַּשָּׁנָה הַבָּאָה
סִדְקֵי הַפְּתָקִים יְהוּ נִפְעָרִים
וְאֶבֶן מִקִּיר תִּזְעַק וְתַדְמִיעַ
לֹא יְפַלֵּל שָׁם אָדָם

עוֹד תִּרְאֶה, בַּשָּׁנָה הַבָּאָה:
זֶה הַכֹּתֶל שֶׁלָּנוּ קוֹרֵס!
מַחֲרִיד מֵרִבְצָם יְשֵׁנֵי הָאֻמָּה
וּנְפֹלֶת גְּוִיּוֹת שׁוּעָלִים צוֹחֲקִים
בֵּין הֲרִיסוֹתָיו
וַאֲנַחְנוּ נֵלֵךְ נֵאָחֵז בִּסְבַךְ־שִׂיחַ אַהֲבוֹתָיו
בַּשָּׁנָה הַבָּאָה, בַּשָּׁנָה הַבָּאָה

You Will Yet See

You will yet see, next year
        above the mountain
        a ruddy cloud will rise
        and its face will be the face of a lion
        all the stones of the mountain, between one watch and the next
        will tremble in the longing roar

You will yet see, next year
        the note-filled crevices will gape
        for a stone shall cry from the wall and shed a tear
        no one will pray there

You will yet see, next year:
        this wall of ours is collapsing!
        frightening from their repose the nation's sleepers
        and the remains of the corpses of laughing foxes
        among its ruins
and we will go in the grasp of the thicket of his loves
        next year, next year

שִׁירִים לְמַעְלָה מֵאֲרִיאֵל

(מתוך פואמה בכתובים)

*

הוֹ אֲרִיאֵל אֲרִיאֵל מַה יָּפְיָפִית
נוֹבוֹ פֶּטֶרְבּוּרְג עַל הָרֵי־בָשֶׂם
אַבִּיר בְּשִׁרְיוֹן אֲנִי
לֹא מַגִּיעַ עָדַיִךְ

אֵילוֹתַיִךְ אֲרִיאֵל בְּלוֹנְד אוּרְבָּנִי
לֹא נִתְפָּסוֹת בָּעֲדָשׁוֹת שֶׁל הַלֵּילוֹת
אֲנִי מֵסִיט אֶת הַתּוֹתָח שֶׁלִּי
אֵלַיִךְ

כּוֹכָבִים נוֹשְׁרִים אֶצְלִי הַלַּיְלָה
כְּנֵסִיּוֹתַיִךְ אֲרִיאֵל פַּעֲמוֹנִים מְדַנְדְּנִים
בַּחֲצוֹת עוֹד מְעַט הַנְּשִׁיקָה

*

עוֹד מְעַט הַנְּשִׁיקָה
וְאַתְּ אֲהוּבָה
רִבּוֹאוֹת קַוִּים רְכוּסִים מִכָּאן
שׁוֹלֵחַ אֶצְבָּעוֹת מִתְאָרְכוֹת לִפְצֹעַ
פְּצָלוֹת בַּלַּיְלָה
לְמַשֵּׁשׁ יְפִי פָּנַיִךְ וְרָאשֵׁי הַיְלָדִים
וּשְׁאֵלוֹת שֶׁפּוֹעֲמוֹת עַכְשָׁו בְּכָרִיּוֹת כַּף הַיָּד

Above Ariel

(from a poem in progress)

*

O Ariel Ariel how beautiful you are
Neuvo Petersburg on scented mountains
an armored knight I
do not reach you

your deer Ariel blond and urban
are not captured in the lenses of the nights
I turn my cannon
toward you

stars are falling near me tonight
your churches Ariel bells chiming
at midnight very soon the kiss

*

soon the kiss
and you beloved
a multitude of lines are ridged from here
I send lengthening fingers to break open
the dark skin of night
to feel the beauty of your face and the heads of the children
and the questions that throb now in the cushions of the palm of the
        hand

(וְאֵיפֹה אַבָּא, וְאִמָּא מַה יִּקְרֶה אִם אַבָּא   )

כְּשֶׁאֶצְבְּעוֹתַי נִפְשָׂקוֹת וּמְנַטְּפוֹת אֶת
יְבָרֶכְךָ הַשֵּׁם וְיִשְׁמְרֶךָ

*

הָיִיתִי רוֹצֶה לְטַיֵּל אִתָּךְ
בַּמְּקוֹמוֹת הָאֲסוּרִים לְטִיּוּל
לְבוֹדְדִים
כָּאן, מֵעֵבֶר לָעַיִן
בֵּין חַמּוּקֵי הָאָרֶץ הַטּוֹבָה
נִרְוֶה דּוֹדִים
חֶלְבָּהּ הַחַם, דִּבְשָׁהּ יְפַעֵם
בַּחֲלָצֵינוּ הַבּוֹעֲרִים לְהִתְעַבֵּר
זֵיתִים שְׁחוֹרִים יִשְׁרוּ עָלֵינוּ
כְּשֶׁנָּבוֹא לְהִתְלַפֵּף בֵּין הַבַּדִּים

*

הוֹ אַחַי מְשׁוֹרְרֵי פָּלַשְׂתִּין
בּוֹאוּ אֵלַי
הַפְשִׁיטוּ מִמֶּנִּי אֶת מַדַּי
וּמֵעַל גּוּפִי הָעֵירֹם
עֲשׂוּ שְׁפָטִים:
בּוֹאִי פָדוּאָה טוּקָאן, בּוֹאִי
תֹּאכְלִי לִי אֶת הַכָּבֵד
וְדָמוֹ הַסָּגֹל טַפְטְפִי עַל הַטֶּרָסוֹת
לְסִימָנֵי דֶּרֶךְ

בּוֹא אֵלַי בּוֹא יָא דַּרְוִויש

(where is daddy, mommy what will happen if daddy)

when my fingers spread and drip
"may the Lord bless you and keep you"

*

I would like to hike with you
in the places where it is forbidden
to hike alone
here, beyond the spring
between the hips of the good land
we lovers will drink our fill of
her warm milk, her honey will throb
in our loins which are burning to conceive
black olives will drop on us
when we come intertwining among the branches

*

O my brothers poets of Palestine
come to me
strip me of my uniform
and on my naked body
        stripe me:
come Fadwa Touqan, come
eat my liver
and drip the purple blood on the terraces
        to mark the way

come to me come Darwish

מִמֶּרְכַּז גּוּפִי
עֲקֹר לִי אֶת הַזַּיִת
שֶׁלְּגַעְגּוּעֶיךָ

*

שַׁבְתִּי וְרָאִיתִי
כָּל הֶחָלָב וְהַדְּבַשׁ
בְּנַעֲרוֹתַיִךְ פָּלַשְׂתִּין בְּנִצַּת שְׁדֵיהֶן בֵּין
הַיְּרֵכַיִם
(הַכֹּל חָתוּם וְנֶאֱנָק בַּאֲרִיגִים כְּבֵדִים)

שַׁבְתִּי וְרָאִיתִי כָּל זֶה בְּזֵיתָא הַכְּפָר בְּפִתְחֵי
בְּאֵרוֹת בְּסִתְרֵי מַדְרֵגוֹת הָיְתָה עָלַי
הַתְּשׁוּקָה

כָּאן, עֶרֶשׂ יַלְדוּתִי
בַּשְּׁבִילִים הַמְעַגְּלִים אֶת הַגְּבָעוֹת

הוֹ אָבִי הוֹ אִמִּי
שֶׁהֲבֵאתֶם אוֹתִי אֶל אֶרֶץ הַזֵּיתִים הַזּוֹ

אֶרוֹס אֶרוֹס אֶרוֹס

*

לֹא מֶלֶךְ לֹא אֵל לֹא גִּבּוֹר
יוֹשִׁיעוּנוּ מִכָּל זֶה

אוּלַי אַהֲבָה
שֶׁרָאִיתִי חֵץ שָׁלוּחַ בֵּין

from the center of my body
uproot from me the olive tree
of your longing

*

I returned and I saw
all the milk and honey
in your girls, Palestine, in the buds of their breasts between
the thighs
(all is sealed and moaning in heavy weaves)

I returned and saw all this in Zeita the village in the openings
of wells in the clefts of the rocks there came upon me
the lust

Here, in the cradle of my childhood
on the paths rounding the hills

O my father O my mother
who brought me to this land of olives

Eros Eros Eros

*

no king no god no hero
will save us from all this

perhaps love
that I saw an arrow extending between

גְרָפִיטִי בִּלָאדִי מִן דָּם וּמִן רוּחַ
בַּקָּצֶה הָאֶחָד עָאסֶם וּמִנֶּגֶד זוּהִירָה
עַל טִיחַ חוֹמָה בְּכִכַּר כִּפְל־חַארֶס
אֵיפֹה קָבוּר יְהוֹשֻׁעַ בִּן־נוּן
הַכּוֹבֵשׁ הַקַּדְמוֹן שֶׁל הָאָרֶץ

graffiti *biladi min dam umin roch*
at one end Assem and at the opposite end Zuhira
on the plaster of the wall in Kifl-Hares Square
burial place of Joshua son of Nun
the ancient conqueror of the land

לַיְלָה בִּירוּשָׁלַיִם

אהבה בהשראת עמיחי

א.
אַתְּ חוֹמָה וְשָׁדַיִךְ
　　בְּאֵרוֹת חָלָב יְצוּקִים שַׁיִשׁ
אֲנִי בְּיִלְלַת תַּנִּים, שׁוֹאֵג כַּלַּיִשׁ
　　מִסְתָּעֵר

ב.
מִבַּעַד לַחַלּוֹן מִגְדַּל דָּוִד מִזְדַּקֵּר
　　שַׁרְבִיט תַּעֲנוּגוֹת מַלְכֵּנוּ הָאָהוּב
לִפְנוֹת בֹּקֶר יָרֵחַ שָׁב לְאֵיתָנוֹ
　　חֲבוּקִים

ג.
בִּבְרֵכוֹת עֵינַיִךְ הַיְּרֻקּוֹת
　　כְּמוֹ נִקְבָּה בָּהָר
אֶטְבֹּל עַצְמִי לָדַעַת
　　שִׁירֵי אַהַב שֶׁשָּׁר

ד.
עַל־יַד בֵּיתוֹ תִּשְׁכַּח
יְמִינִי אִם לֹא אֶזְכְּרֵכִי
　　אֵיךְ הֵם אָהֲבוּ יֹאמְרוּ
בֵּינוֹת לָאֲבָנִים הָעַתִּיקוֹת
　　עֵינוֹת הַמַּיִם
שָׁמַיִם מִתְקַנְּאִים בָּנוּ עַכְשָׁו

Night in Jerusalem

LOVE INSPIRED BY AMICHAI

a.
you are a wall and your breasts
        wells of milk cast in marble
I, at the howling of the jackals, roar like a lion
        charging

b.
at the window the Tower of David stands out
        the scepter of pleasures of our beloved king
towards morning a moon regains its strength
        embracing

c.
in the green pools of your eyes
        as in a mountain conduit
I will immerse myself to know
        the love songs he sang

d.
near his house may my right hand
be forsaken if I do not remember thee
        how they loved they will say
among the ancient stones
        the springs of water
heaven envies us now

*

יוֹשֵׁב בָּאוֹטוֹבּוּס הַמִּתְקַתֵּק
לְהִתְפּוֹצֵץ
וְכוֹתֵב אֶת שִׁירִי הָאַחֲרוֹן.
עוֹד מְעַט יִתְאַבֵּךְ הַכֹּל וְיַעֲלֶה בִּסְעָרָה כְּרֶכֶב אֵשׁ
וְנִהְיֶה מְפֻזָּרִים לְכָל הָעֲבָרִים וְנִהְיֶה אֶחָד
וְנִתְעַשֵּׁן לַעֲנָנִים דַּקִּים בִּרְקִיעַ הַשָּׁמַיִם וַחֲבוּרִים
לָעֲשָׁנִים מִן הַיָּמִים הָאֲחֵרִים

לְמַטָּה וַדַּאי תִּבַכִּי אוֹתִי
וְקִינָה תִּנָּשֵׂא וּנְהִי
כְּשֶׁאַחַד הַמְשׁוֹרְרִים (אוֹ הָרַבָּנִים) יְצַוַּח בְּקוֹל מַר כַּשּׁוֹפָר:
אֵי הַלָּשׁוֹן הַמְמַהֶרֶת בְּאִמְרֵי שֶׁפֶר
לוֹחֶכֶת עַתָּה אֶת הָאַסְפַלְט

בְּטֶרֶם יִסְתְּמוּ הַגּוֹלֵל תִּקְרְאִי לְפָנַי
אֶת שִׁירִי זֶה הָאַחֲרוֹן

וּבְכִי חֲרִישִׁי יָזוּב עַד הָעוֹלָם

*

Sitting on the bus which is ticking
to explode
writing my last poem.
Soon all will grow hazy and ascend stormily like a chariot of fire
and we will be scattered all over and we will be one
and we will rise as smoke into thin clouds in the heavens uniting
with the smoke of other days

down below you will surely mourn for me
and an elegy will be delivered and a dirge
when one of the poets (or the rabbis) will shout in a voice bitter as
the shofar:
how the tongue so quick with fine words
now licks the asphalt

before the grave is sealed read before me
this last poem of mine

and a silent weeping will run forever

eace is stained with blood not only the song of peace is stained with blood not only the

מַשֶׁהוּ עוֹד יָקוּם

מַשֶׁהוּ עוֹד יָקוּם מִתּוֹךְ כָּל הַדָּם הַזֶּה
אֲנִי יוֹדֵעַ
לֹא עוֹד יֶהֱמֶה הַתַּנִּין הַגָּדוֹל צַחֲנָתוֹ
כְּשֶׁעוֹף בָּרְקִיעִים יָשׁוּב לְשׁוֹרֵר

מַשֶׁהוּ עוֹד יָקוּם מִתּוֹךְ כָּל הַדָּם הַזֶּה
וּמִי שֶׁשָּׁתָה דָּם לְשִׁכָּרוֹן – וְנָמַסּוּ הָרִים
מִדָּמוֹ

מַשֶׁהוּ עוֹד יָקוּם מִתּוֹךְ כָּל הַדָּם הַזֶּה
אוּלַי שִׁירִים, אֲנִי אוֹמֵר, מְנֻקָּבִים
אֶרֶץ אַל תְּכַסִּי
(זֶה חֲתַן הַדָּמִים שֶׁנִּכְנַס לִי בִּפְנִים)

מַשֶׁהוּ עוֹד יָקוּם מִתּוֹךְ כָּל הַדָּם הַזֶּה
אֲנִי רוֹאֶה
כְּסוּת אַרְגָּמָן שֶׁלַּמָּשִׁיחַ עוֹלָה

מַשֶׁהוּ עוֹד יָקוּם מִתּוֹךְ כָּל הַדָּם הַזֶּה
פִּתְאֹם, בַּבֹּקֶר בַּבֹּקֶר, עַם
וַיִּתְחִיל לָלֶכֶת

מַשֶׁהוּ עוֹד יָקוּם מִתּוֹךְ כָּל הַדָּם הַזֶּה
(וּכְדִבְרֵי הַנָּבִיא – בְּדָמַיִךְ חֲיִי)
בֵּינְתַיִם
פַּחַד בְּכוֹרוֹת לוֹטֵף אוֹתִי בְּכָל לַיְלָה
בַּחֲצוֹת

Something Will Rise Yet

Something will rise yet out of all this blood
I know
no longer will the great crocodile raise his shout
when a bird in the heavens sings again

Something will rise yet out of all this blood
and who became drunk on blood – and mountains melted
from his blood

Something will rise yet from all this blood
perhaps poems, I say, punctured
O earth, cover not

(it's the bridegroom of blood that has entered me)

Something will rise yet from all this blood
I see
a crimson garment of the Messiah rising

Something will rise yet from all this blood
suddenly, early in the morning, a nation
and it will start to walk

Something will rise yet from all this blood
(and as the prophet said – in your blood, live)
in the meantime
the terror of the first born caresses me each night
at midnight

*

וּפִתְאֹם פָּרַץ אָבִיב בְּאֶמְצַע
הַמַּרְחֶשְׁוָן הַזֶּה
וְרָאִיתִי הַחַיָּל הַיָּפֶה (לִפְנֵי שֶׁנִּבְלַעְתִּי בְּפִי הַמִּנְהָרָה)
שָׁעוּן עַל אֶבֶן הַמַּחְסוֹם הַגְּדוֹלָה בִּתְנוּחַת הַכּוֹבֵשׁ הָרַךְ

וּמִי יוּכַל לְגַל אֶת שְׁרַב־הַסְּתָו, אֶת
הַחַיָּל וְאֶת הָאֶבֶן הַגְּדוֹלָה מִפִּי
הָאָרֶץ הַמְצַעֶקֶת הַזּוֹ

*

and suddenly spring burst forth in the middle
    of this MarCheshvan
and I saw the beautiful soldier (before I was swallowed into the mouth
    of the tunnel)
leaning on the large stone barrier, in the pose of a gentle conqueror

O who can roll the autumn heat
    the soldier and the huge stone off the mouth
        of this screaming land

עֲקוּדִים

וּכְמוֹ פַּעַם בִּירוּשָׁלֶם
בְּגוּשׁ חָלָב וּמְצָדָה
הָיִינוּ אָנוּ:
עֲקוּדִים נְקוּדִים וְיוֹקְדִים מִתַּבְעֵרַת
אֱלֹהֵינוּ זֶה שָׁלֹשׁ שָׁנִים

כָּאן, אֶרֶץ תַּלְאוּבָה וּנְקוּבָה
הַרְחֵק מִמַּלְכוּת הַשָּׁמַיִם
מַה נַּעַשׂ לְאֱלְקַנָּא הַזֶּה
מַלְכֵּנוּ וְאָבִינוּ, לֹא נַתִּיר שֶׁכָּךְ
לֹא נַתִּיר עַצְמֵנוּ מִן הַסֶּלַע, אוּלַי
יַחֲזֹר
לֹא נַתִּיר, עִמּוֹ אֲנַחְנוּ בַּצָּרָה, לֹא
נַתִּיר עֲקֵדָתֵנוּ אֵלָיו בִּרְצוּעוֹת
הַשָּׁחוֹר

עַד יִשְׁלַח הַמַּלְאָךְ

The Bound Ones

And as it was once in Jerusalem
in Gush Chalav and Massada
we were:
striped speckled and burning from the conflagration
of our God these three years

Here, an arid pocked land
far from the kingdom of heaven
what shall we do to this jealous God
our King our Father, we will not permit this
we will not release ourselves from the rock, perhaps he will return
we will not release, we will be with him in woe, we will not
release the black straps of our sacrificial binding to him

until he sends the angel

מֵחֶבְלֵי מָשִׁיחַ

מָשִׁיחַ
בֶּן
דָּוִד
נֶאֱפֶה
בְּרֶחֶם
יָרֵחַ
בְּגוֹן
אֲפַרְסֵק
תָּלוּי
וּמִתְנוֹדֵד
מֵעַל
הֲרָרַיִךְ
אֶפְרָת
אֲנִי
קוֹרֵא
לוֹ
בּוֹא
מָשִׁיחַ
בּוֹא בּוֹא
מָשִׁיחַ
עַד
מָתַי
תְּהֵא
מִתְמַהְמֵהַּ
עַד
בּוֹא
מָשִׁיחַ

אֱלֹהִים
מְגָרֵר
מָשִׁיחַ
בִּפְתוֹתֵי
הַשֶּׁלֶג
חוֹבֵשׁ
פְּצָעַיִךְ
מְצַנֵּן
לִבִּי
מִן הַמִּכְוָה
מְעַט
שַׁלְוָה
כְּשֶׁבְּנִי
בְּכוֹרִי
אֲחִיָּה
אוֹמֵר לִי
שֶׁכְּפַר עֶצְיוֹן
הַיּוֹם
כַּלָּה
וְהָעֲקֵבוֹת שֶׁלָּנוּ
יַהֲלוֹמִים
עַל
הַשִּׂמְלָה

Pre-Messianic Pangs

Messiah
son of
David
baked in
womb
peach
hued
moon
hanging
swinging
above
your mountains
Efrat
I
call
to him
come
Messiah
come come
Messiah
until
when
will you
tarry
until the
coming of
the Messiah

God
grates
Messiah
to snow
flakes
dresses
your wounds
cools
the scorch of
my heart
a bit of
serenity
when my
first born
son
Achia
tells me
that Kfar Etzion
today
is a bride
and our footprints
are diamonds
on
her dress

שׁוּב מוֹכְרִים

שׁוּב מוֹכְרִים אוֹתִי, אֲנִי
בַּעַל־הַחֲלוֹמוֹת שֶׁרָאִיתִי הַשֶּׁמֶשׁ הַיָּרֵחַ וְאַחַד־עָשָׂר
הַכּוֹכָבִים מִשְׁתַּחֲוִים
אֲנִי יָכוֹל לְהִתְרָעֵד אֵיךְ שֶׁהַכֹּל חוֹזֵר:
הַלְּפִיתָה, קְרִיעַת הַכְּתֹנֶת מֵעַל הַבָּשָׂר
הַהַשְׁלָכָה הַרְחֵק אֶל חֵיק הַנְּחָשִׁים
גַּם הֵם הָלְכוּ רָחוֹק הַפַּעַם, הָאַחִים,
אֱלֵי ז'נֶב ז'נֶב כַּמָּה מָתוֹק לְגַלְגֵּל שְׁמֵךְ ז'נֶב
זוֹנַת הֶעָרִים וְהַמְּדִינוֹת

מוֹכְרִים אוֹתִי וְגַם אֶת הַמָּקוֹם
בּוֹ נָשְׁקוּ שִׂפְתֵי הָאֱלֹהִים אֶת בֶּטֶן
הָעָם הַזֶּה (כַּעֲרֵמַת־חִטִּים,
אָמַר מְשׁוֹרֵר אַחֵר, בַּגֹּרֶן בְּלֵיל לְבָנָה)

אֲבָל הִשְׁאִירוּ לָנוּ אֶת הַפָּאלוֹס הַמַּלְכוּתִי
מִגְדַּל דָּוִד הַמִּזְדַּקֵּר וּבִקְצֵה (כְּמוֹ עָגִיל) לוֹ
שַׁבְרִיַּת־סַהַר־הָאִסְלָם
לַיְלָה אֶחָד אֶתְלַטֵּף עָלָיו וְאֶעֶקְרֶנּוּ
אָז זִרְמַת־הַכּוֹכָבִים שֶׁתִּיָּרֶה
תַּרְוֶה שְׁבִילֵי־חָלָב רַעֲנַנִּים שֶׁבָּרָקִיעַ כֹּה יִהְיֶה זַרְעֵנוּ

Selling Again

They are selling me again, me
the dreamer who saw the sun and the moon and the eleven
stars bowing down
I can shudder the way everything comes back:
the grasping, the shirt being ripped off of the flesh
the casting far into the midst of the snakes
they too went too far this time, the brothers,
to Geneve Geneve how sweet to roll your name Geneve
whore of cities and countries

They are selling me and also the place
where the lips of God kissed the belly
of this nation (like a heap of wheat,
said another poet, on the threshing floor on a moonlit night)

but they left us the royal phallus
the prominent Tower of David and on the top (like an earring)
the *shabria* knife of Islam
one night I will cuddle against it, breaking it off
then the star-flow that will be ejaculated
will fill fresh milky ways in the heavens so will be our seed

הזמנה לבכי

שישה שירים על ההתנתקות

"זֶהוּ קֶרַע חָדָשׁ בְּפָרֹכֶת הַבְּרִית!
מִי יוֹדֵעַ אִם עוֹד יִמָּצֵא בְּדוֹרִי
אָמַּן־הָאִחוּי, מִי יוֹדֵעַ. אֲבוֹי!"

אורי צבי גרינברג, כרוניקה שחורה / קרע הברית
תרצ"ג-תרצ"ד, בתוך ספר הקטרוג והאמונה

לכל אותם העקורים והעוקרים
שפעלו למען לא ייהפך לנו
קרע הבית
לקרע הברית

An Invitation to Cry

Six Poems on the Dissociation

"This is a new tear in the curtain of the covenant!
Who knows if in my generation will be found
A healing-master, who knows, woe!"

Uri Zvi Greenberg, "Black Chronicle / the Renting of the Covenant" 5693–5694, in The Book of Accusation and Faith

To all the dispossessed and the dispossessors
who acted to prevent the tearing of the house
from becoming the tearing of the covenant

הַזְמָנָה לְבֶכִי

אֵלֶיךָ הַחַיָּל הַטּוֹב הַנֶּאֱמָן שֶׁבְּיוֹם מִן הַיָּמִים הוּא יוֹם פְּקֻדָּה
תִּקְרַב לִמְעוֹנֵנוּ:

אָרוּץ אֵלֶיךָ בִּזְרוֹעוֹת פְּתוּחוֹת אָרוּץ אֲחַבֶּקְךָ וְאוֹבִילְךָ
לִפְנֵי הַפֶּתַח אֹחַז צַוְּארוֹנְךָ, אֶקְרַע בְּךָ קְרִיעָה עַד
מְקוֹם הַלֵּב

תִּכָּנֵס, תֵּשֵׁב עִמָּנוּ בִּישִׁיבַת הָאֲבֵלִים, תִּטְעַם הַכְּעָכִים הָעֲגֻלִּים
כְּמוֹ הַיְלָדִים שֶׁגַּם עַכְשָׁו מִתְגַּלְגְּלִים עַל הַשָּׁטִיחַ כְּמוֹ
גּוֹרָל, שׁוּב הוֹפְכִים בָּתִּים בְּעֶצְיוֹן לִנְקוּבִים וַחֲלוּלִים

בִּדְמָמָה נֵלֵךְ בָּאַחֲרוֹנָה בֵּין חַדְרֵי הַבַּיִת:
רַק אֲנִי וְאַתְּ וְהַכְּתָלִים זוֹכְרִים רִיבִים וַאֲהָבִים
שׁוּרוֹת שֶׁנִּכְתְּבוּ שֶׁנִּמְחֲקוּ כְּמוֹ נִכְווֹת בְּסֵפֶר הַחַיִּים
בְּעֵינֶיךָ, חַיָּלִי הַטּוֹב, אֶרְאֶה דִּמְעָה, רֵעֵינוּ חוֹנְקִים אֶת
בִּכְיָם, כָּתַב בְּתַשַׁ"ח הַמְשׁוֹרֵר, עַכְשָׁו אוּלַי מֻתָּר לִבְכּוֹת
וְאִם הָיָה עוֹד זְמַן
הָיִינוּ רוֹבְצִים בִּנְאוֹת דֶּשֶׁא וְשׁוּב מְשַׂחֲקִים
בְּמִשְׂחַק הַמַּחֲבוֹאִים שֶׁל
שִׁיר הַשִּׁירִים
אַתְּ הָרַעְיָה, אֲנִי הַדּוֹד, אַתָּה בְּתַפְקִיד הַשּׁוֹמְרִים

וְהָיִיתִי בְּרִיצָה לוֹקֵחַ אוֹתְךָ מֵעַל לְבֵית הַקְּבָרוֹת –
לְכָאן, בִּשְׁעַת רַעֲוָא דְּרַעֲוִין אַחַת
שָׁמַעְתִּי תְּפִלְּלַת הַמּוּאַזִּין כִּתְפִלַּת יְהוּדָאִין יַחַד עוֹלוֹת

An Invitation to Cry

To you the good loyal soldier who on that day the day of the order
will approach our dwelling:

I will run to you with open arms I will run I will embrace you and
lead you.
In front of the entrance I will take hold of your collar, I will tear it to
the place where your heart is

Enter, sit with us, the mourners, taste the round pretzels
like the children who even now are tumbling on the rug like
fate, again houses in Etzion are turning pocked and hollow

Silently we will walk at the end through the rooms of the house:
Only I and you, my wife, and the walls remember quarrels and loving,
lines that were written and erased as though burned into the book
of life.
In your eyes, my good soldier, I will see a tear. Our friends stifle
their crying, wrote the poet in 1948, perhaps now it is permitted to cry
and if there were more time
we would lie down in green pastures and play again
the hide-and-seek game of
the Song of Songs
you as my love, I as the beloved. And you, soldier, in the role of the
watchmen

and I would take you running above the cemetery –
to here, in an hour of great favor
I heard the *allah* of the muezzin
as though rising together with the praying of *yehudain*

כָּאן אֶפְשָׁר לְהִתְנַבֵּא, כָּאן
אִם רַק הָיָה לָנוּ עוֹד זְמַן

בִּלְחִישָׁה אַתָּה שׁוֹאֵל: אֲרַזְתֶּם? כְּאִלּוּ יֵשׁ בְּזֶה הָעוֹלָם הַצְּרוֹר
שֶׁכֹּה יָכִיל גַּעְגּוּעִים

אַתָּה עוֹצֵר בְּשֶׁטֶף הַדְּמָעוֹת. יוֹצְאִים לְנְשֹׁם עַל הַמִּרְפֶּסֶת
כָּאן הֵכַנְתִּי לִי פִּנָּה קְטַנָּה לִכְתֹּב אֶת הָרוֹמָן הַלֹּא גָּמוּר
עַכְשָׁו מֵעֵץ הַתְּאֵנָה שֶׁבֶּחָצֵר עָלֶה אַחֲרוֹן נוֹשֵׁר
הַכֹּל מָלֵא סְמָלִים אַתָּה אוֹמֵר
נוֹפֵל עַל צַוָּארִי בִּבְכִי וּמְמָרֵר
חַיָּלִי הַנֶּאֱמָן, הַטּוֹב, עַכְשָׁו מֻתָּר סוֹף סוֹף לִבְכּוֹת.

(מפחד לב יומם, שבט התשס"ה בכפר עציון)

here one can prophesy, here
if only we had more time

in a whisper you ask: have you packed? as though there were in this world a bundle
which can contain yearning

You hold back the stream of tears. We go out for a breath of air on the porch
here I prepared a little corner to write the unfinished novel
now from the fig tree in the yard the last leaf falls
everything is filled with symbols you say
you fall on my neck, weeping bitterly
my good, loyal soldier, now at long last it is permitted to cry.

(with daytime anxiety, Shevat 5765, in Kfar Etzion)

הָאָרֶץ הַזֹּאת שֶׁרוֹעֶדֶת לָנוּ מִתַּחַת לָרַגְלַיִם

הָאָרֶץ הַזֹּאת שֶׁרוֹעֶדֶת לָנוּ מִתַּחַת לָרַגְלַיִם הִיא
לְבִיאָה מִשְׁתּוֹלֶלֶת.
הִיא כְּבָר זְמַן לְבִיאָה מִשְׁתּוֹלֶלֶת צוֹעֶקֶת פְּצָעֶיהָ
מִן הַפְּטָמוֹת רוֹצִים לַעֲקֹר לָהּ אֶת הַגּוּרִים
עַכְשָׁו שַׁאֲגָתָהּ מִתְגַּלְגֶּלֶת

הָאָרֶץ הַזֹּאת שֶׁרוֹעֶדֶת לָנוּ מִתַּחַת לָרַגְלַיִם
תְּנַעֵר אוֹתָנוּ (כְּמוֹ שָׁטִיחַ אֶת הָאָבָק לִפְנֵי הַפֶּסַח)
רַק מִי שֶׁצּוּמוּד בְּנַפְשׁוֹ יִוָּתֵר

הָאָרֶץ הַזֹּאת שֶׁרוֹעֶדֶת לָנוּ מִתַּחַת לָרַגְלַיִם בַּיּוֹם הַהוּא תִּבָּקַע
מִצְּפוֹן יָם־הַמֶּלַח תָּזוּב בַּנָּהָר הַסָּמִיךְ שֶׁל חָלָב וּדְבַשׁ
בִּנְהַר הֶחָלָב וְהַדְּבַשׁ שֶׁיַּדְבִּיק אוֹתָנוּ אֵלָיו
כְּמִנְהַג כָּל הַנְּהָרוֹת
אֱלֵי יָם

שבט תשס"ד

This Land Trembling Under Our Feet

This land trembling under our feet is
a wild lioness.
For some time now she is a wild lioness screaming her wounds
from the nipples they want to uproot her cubs
now her roar rolls on

this land trembling under our feet
will shake us (like a rug its dust before Passover)
only those who are *tsumud* in their souls will remain

this land trembling under our feet on that day will split
from the northern Dead Sea she will ooze in a dense river of milk
and honey
in the milk and honey river that will adhere us to it
as is the custom of all rivers
to the sea

Shevat, 5764

מוֹת הַלִּוְיָתָן

"לִוְיָתָן זֶה־יָצַרְתָּ לְשַׂחֶק־בּוֹ"
(תהלים קד)

לֹא עוֹד תִּשְׁמַע צְפִירַת גַּעְגּוּעֶיךָ, יֶלֶד לִוְיָתָן
לֹא עוֹד.
מֵאֵיזוֹ תְּהוֹם עָשִׂיתָ עֲלִיָּה?
לֹא יָדַעְתָּ שֶׁבַּצַּד הָאָפֵל שֶׁל אֶרֶץ שְׁכוּרַת־שֶׁמֶשׁ זוֹ
רַב הַצַּלְמָוֶת?
לֹא שָׁמַעְתָּ כִּי כָּאן אֶרֶץ אוֹכֶלֶת יְלָדֶיהָ?
מֵרֹאשׁ הַכַּרְמֶל הָאִי־נִרְאֶה הָעוֹלֶה בְּעָשָׁן
רוֹאֶה אוֹתְךָ, יֶלֶד לִוְיָתָן
חוֹתֵר אֶל הַכָּחֹל הַכָּחֹל וְלֹא יָכוֹל. וּמַה
בִּקַּשְׁתָּ לְהָבִיא בִּסְנַפִּירֶיךָ? אוּלַי מְעַט שַׁלְוַת אוֹקְיָנוֹס
אוֹ פַנְטַזְיַת כָּל אָדָם לְהִבָּלַע כְּמוֹ פִּינוֹקְיוֹ אוֹ יוֹנָה
בָּרֶחֶם הַגְּדוֹלָה?
אוּלַי הֶמְיַת־אַלְפַּיִם־שְׁנוֹת עָשְׁתָה דַּרְכָּהּ בְּקוֹל צְפִירַת גַּעְגּוּעֶיךָ...
וְעַכְשָׁו אַתָּה יוֹדֵעַ, כְּמוֹ דָּוִד בִּתְהִלִּים, כֻּלָּנוּ כְּלֵי־מִשְׂחָק
בְּיַד הָאֱלֹהִים
וְאֵין לִי לֵב לָשׁוּב לִרְאוֹת אוֹתְךָ עוֹד מִטַּלְטֵל
בְּתוֹךְ גַּלֵּי־תִּקְוָה־קְטַנִּים
בְּמֵי הַקִּישׁוֹן הַמְכַלִּים.

ניסן תשס"ה

The Death of the Whale

"leviathan, whom thou hast made to play therein"
PSALMS 104

No longer will be heard your yearning hoot, whale child
no longer.
From what depths did you make aliyah?
Didn't you know that on the dark side of this sun-drunk land
the deathshadow is great?
Have you not heard that here is a land that devours its children?
From the top of the invisible Mount Carmel which is going up in smoke
I see you, whale child
crawling to the blue the blue unsuccessfully. What
did you want to bring with your fins? Perhaps a bit of ocean tranquility
or everyone's fantasy to be swallowed like Pinochio or Jonah
into the giant womb?
Perhaps a 2000 year longing made its way in the sound of your yearning hoot...
And now you know, like David in the Psalms, we are all pawns
in the hands of God
and I don't have the heart to see you again in the throes
of little-hope-waves
in the destructive waters of the Kishon river.

Nisan 5765

שִׁירִים שֶׁנִּכְתְּבוּ בַּחוֹל [א]

בְּרֹגֶז – דָּמִים תִּזְכֹּר
בְּרֹגֶז – עֲקֵדָה תִּזְכֹּר
וּמִי גְדוֹלָה מִמִּי:
טַלִּי וְאַרְבַּע בְּנוֹתֶיהָ אוֹ
חַנָּה וְשִׁבְעַת בָּנֶיהָ?
אֵל אֱלֹהֵי אִמָּהוֹת

*

אֵל אֱלֹהֵי אִמָּהוֹת וְאָבוֹת
בְּרֹגֶז רַגְלַיִם תִּזְכֹּר
רַגְלֵי פִּרְחֵי כֹּהֲנִים נִקְטְמוּ
כְּקוֹצִים כְּסוּחִים
אֶצְבָּעוֹת לֹא עוֹד יַטְבִּיעוּ רֵיחָן
בַּחוֹלוֹת הַיָּפִים

*

טוֹבִים הָיוּ לִי חוֹלוֹת קָטִיף
מֵאַלְפֵי זָהָב וָכֶסֶף
גַּם לְשׁוֹנוֹת רַבָּנָן וְתַלְמִידֵיהוֹן
זָכוּ לְלַחֵךְ כָּאן הֶעָפָר

*

וְשׁוּב אֲנִי יֶלֶד־חוֹלוֹת מְחַפֵּשׂ עֲקֵבוֹת
כָּאן פַּעַם – גְּרָר
אַבְרָהָם וְיִצְחָק, וְרַק אֵין יִרְאַת אֱלֹהִים בַּמָּקוֹם הַזֶּה
וַהֲרָגוּנִי

Poems Written in the Sand [a]

In anger – remember blood
In anger – remember sacrificial binding
And who is greater:
Tali and her four daughters or
Hanna and her seven sons?
Great God of mothers

*

Great God of mothers and fathers
in anger remember feet
the feet of novice priests were cut off
like mowed weeds
toes will no longer impress their smell
in the beautiful sands

*

they were good to me, the sands of Katif,
more than abundant gold and silver
the tongues of the Rabbis and their students too
got to lick the dirt here

*

and once again I am a child-of-the-sands searching for footprints
here once – Grar
Abraham and Isaac, surely there is no fear of God in this place
and they will kill me

*

רָאִיתִי הַיָּם מְקוֹנֵן בְּשִׁירַת הַיָּם
פִּסָּה שֶׁל הַכָּחֹל הַזֶּה נִקְרַעַת
מֵעֵינַי
בְּחוֹמַת הַבֶּטוֹן
בְּבַת־יַלְדָּה נִסְחֶפֶת לַחוֹף. כָּל מִשְׁבָּרֶיךָ וְגַלֶּיךָ
וּכְמוֹ אָז, בַּשִּׁירָה
הַשֵּׁם יִמְלֹךְ לְעוֹלָם וָעֶד

*

לִכְתֹּב עַל הַחוֹף כְּתֹבֶת חוֹל גְּדוֹלָה:
"ארץ ישראל שייכת לעם ישראל"
לְקַשֵּׁט בִּצְדָפִים וּבְקוֹנְכִיּוֹת
וְלִצְפּוֹת מֵהַצַּד
אֵיךְ שֶׁגַּל מַקְצִיף וְגָדוֹל
מוֹחֶה הַכֹּל

פסח תשס"ה

*

I saw the sea lamenting in the Song of the Sea
a piece of this blue is torn
from my eyes
by a concrete wall
a girl doll is swept to the shore. All your breakers and your waves
and as then, in the Song
The Lord will rule forever

*

write on the sand a huge inscription:
"THE LAND OF ISRAEL BELONGS TO THE PEOPLE OF
ISRAEL"
decorate it with sea shells
and observe from the side
how a big frothy wave
erases everything

Passover 5765

שִׁירִים שֶׁנִּכְתְּבוּ בַּחוֹל [ב]

בְּרֹגֶז – רַחֵם תִּזְכֹּר
בְּרֹגֶז – תְּמִימוּת תִּזְכֹּר
רַחֵם – כְּזוֹ הַתְּכֵלֶת
תְּמִימוּת – כְּזֶה הַחוֹל
שֶׁמָּא יָשׁוּב וִיכַּס אֶת הַכֹּל

*

כְּזֶה הַחוֹל
שֶׁלֹּא יִגָּמֵר לְעוֹלָם

*

שֶׁלֹּא יִסָּפֵר מֵרֹב

*

בְּטַח בְּהַשֵּׁם וַעֲשֵׂה־
טוֹב
שְׁכָן־אֶרֶץ וּרְעֵה אֱמוּנָה
תּוֹרַת הַשֵּׁם תְּ מִי מָה מְשִׁיבַת נָפֶשׁ
מִזְמוֹר לְדָוִד – הַשֵּׁם מִי־יָגוּר בְּאָהֳלֶךָ
מִי־יִשְׁכֹּן בְּהַר קָדְשֶׁךָ
הוֹלֵךְ תָּ מִ ים וּפֹעֵל צֶדֶק
וְדֹבֵר אֱמֶת בִּלְבָבוֹ.

(כתובות מארון הקודש
של בית הכנסת בגני טל)

Poems Written in the Sand [b]

In anger – remember mercy
In anger – remember innocence
Mercy – like this azure
Innocence – like this sand
Perhaps it will return and cover everything

*

like this sand
which will never end

*

which may not be numbered for multitude

*

Trust in the LORD, and do
good;
so you will dwell in the land, and enjoy security.
the precepts of the LORD are right, rejoicing the heart
A Psalm of David – O LORD, who shall sojourn in thy tent?
Who shall dwell on thy holy hill?
He who walks blamelessly, and does what is right,
and speaks truth from his heart.

(inscription from the holy ark
of the synagogue in Ganei Tal)

כָּזֶה חֹק הַתְּמִימוּת רָאִיתִי
וּבָכִיתִי

*

רָאִיתִי תַּמִּים מַאֲמִינִים וְזוֹרְעִים
מִי יִתְקַע לְכַפְּךָ הַזּוֹרֵעַ
כִּי בְּרִנָּה תִּקְצֹר

*

אֲנִי אוֹמֵר (בְּשֶׁקֶט, בַּלֵּב פְּנִימָה)
שֶׁמָּא יְכַס הַחוֹל
הַיָּם יֶהוֹם
וְאַתָּה זוֹרֵעַ

*

אֵלִי – שֶׁלֹּא יִגָּמֵר לְעוֹלָם:
הַחוֹל וְהַיָּם הַחוֹל וְהַיָּם הַחוֹל
וְהַיָּם

*

תְּפִלַּת הָאָדָם:
מָלְאוּ אֲסָמֵינוּ בָּר, בָּתֵּינוּ תִּינוֹקוֹת
מָה עוֹד תְּבַקְשִׁי מֵאִתָּנוּ
מְכוֹרָה

*

שִׁלַּמְנוּ בְּחֵלֶב שִׁלַּמְנוּ בְּדָם שִׁלַּמְנוּ בְּדֶמַע שִׁלַּמְנוּ בְּיֶזַע
בְּמוֹרַג חָרוּץ נָכִין בַּחוֹלוֹת לִזְרָעִים חֲדָשִׁים

so I saw the law of naiveté
and wept

*

I saw the naive believing and sowing
who will shake your sowing hand to seal an agreement
that you will reap in joy

*

I say (quietly, inside the heart)
perhaps the sand will cover
the sea will roil
and you are sowing

*

my God – may it never end:
the sand and the sea the sand and the sea the sand
and the sea

*

The prayer of man:
Our barns are filled with grain, our houses with infants
what more will you ask of us
sold homeland

*

we paid with fat we paid with blood we paid with tears we paid with
sweat
in the cracked threshing sledge we will prepare in the sand for new
seeds

*

עַכְשָׁו אֲנִי אוֹמֵר (כִּמְעַט יוֹדֵעַ)
עוֹד כָּל יְמֵי הָאָרֶץ, גַּם בַּחוּלוֹת הָאֵלֶּה
זֶרַע וְקָצִיר
וְקֹר וָחֹם
וְקַיִץ וָחֹרֶף
וְיוֹם וָלַיְלָה

לֹא יִשְׁבֹּתוּ

אייר־סיון תשס"ה

*

now I say (almost know)
for all the days of the land, in these sands too
seed and harvest
and cold and heat
and summer and winter
and day and night

will not cease

Iyar-Sivan 5765

שִׁירִים שֶׁנִּכְתְּבוּ בַּחוֹל [ג]

"קְחוּ אֶת מֵתֵיכֶם וְשׁוּבוּ לְאַרְצוֹתֵיכֶם
לַמְּקוֹמוֹת שֶׁמֵּהֶם בָּאתֶם."
(מחמוד דרויש)

בְּרֹגֶז – דָּמִים תִּזְכֹּר
בְּרֹגֶז – תְּמִימוּת תִּזְכֹּר
בְּרֹגֶז – עֲקֵדָה תִּזְכֹּר
תְּמִימוּת – כְּאֵלֶּה הַחַיִּים מִמַּעַל לַחוֹלוֹת
דָּמִים – כְּאֵלֶּה הַמֵּתִים
גַּם לָהֶם אֵין כָּאן מְנוּחָה

*

הִנֵּה־הִנָּם מֵתֵי קָטִיף:
יָפִים וְזוֹהֲרִים אֲנִי רוֹאָם בְּלֵיל
תְּשִׁיעִי שֶׁל אָב
אוֹחֲזִים יָדַיִם
מְבַכִּים אֶת הַחַיִּים
כְּשֶׁנֹּגַהּ לְבָנָה נִשְׁפָּךְ בֵּין הַחוֹלוֹת
הֵם לוֹחֲשִׁים:
הַאָמְנָם תּוֹצִיאוּנוּ כָּעֵת
הַאָמְנָם

*

הִנֵּה אֶחָד מֵהֶם – יוֹחָנָן לוֹ פְּנֵי־מַלְאָךְ
שׁוֹלֵחַ יָד וּמַעֲמִיק הַחֲתִירָה
אֶל הַמִּזְרָח

Poems Written in the Sand [c]

"Take your dead and return to your lands
to the places from which you came."
(MAHMOUD DARWISH)

In anger – remember blood
In anger – remember innocence
In anger – remember sacrificial binding
Innocence – like those living above the sands
Blood – like the dead
Even they have no rest here

*

here they are the dead of Katif:
beautiful and shining, I saw them on the night
of the ninth of Av
holding hands
lamenting the living
when the moon glow spills among the sands
they whisper:
will you indeed remove us now
will you indeed

*

behold one of them – Angel-faced Yochanan
reaches out and deepens the digging
to the east

אֶל יְשֵׁנֵי חֶבְרוֹן וְאֶל רָחֵל וְאֶל
יוֹסֵף שֶׁבַּשּׁוֹמְרוֹן
הֵם וַדַּאי יוֹדְעִים דָּבָר אוֹ שְׁנַיִם
עַל עֲקֵידָה
וְעַל בָּנִים שָׁבִים וְעַל גּוֹלִים

*

בְּלֵיל תְּשִׁיעִי שֶׁל אָב עוֹמֵד בְּסֶלַע עֶצְיוֹן
וְחוֹלוֹת נוֹדְדִים תַּחְתַּי
בֵּין הַחַיִּים וּבֵין הַמֵּתִים קְטֹרֶת שִׁירַי
בְּיָדַי
הַמַּגֵּפָה לֹא נֶעֱצֶרֶת

*

מִכָּאן אֲנִי מַשְׁקִיף עַל לוּחַ הַזְּמַנִּים וְרוֹאֶה
הַכֹּל נֶחְטָף בְּט"ו בְּאָב
הַבְּתוּלוֹת וְהַכְּרָמִים וְהַמְּחוֹלוֹת הָעֲלָמִים
הַבָּתִּים וְהַגַּנִּים וְהַחַיִּים וְהַמֵּתִים
הַכֹּל נִטְרָף

וְלֹא הָיוּ יָמִים טוֹבִים לְיִשְׂרָאֵל

ליל תשעה באב, תשס"ה

to the dead of Hebron to Rachel and to
        Joseph who is in Samaria
they surely know a thing or two
        about sacrificial binding
        and about returning sons and about exiles

*

on the night of the ninth of Av I stand on the rock of Etzion
        and sands shift under me
between the living and the dead the incense of my poems
        is in my hands
the plague does not cease

*

from here I look at the timetable and see
        everything is snatched on Tu B'Av
the virgins and the vineyards and the dances the young men
        the houses and the gardens and the living and the dead
everything is preyed upon

and there were no better days for Israel

The eve of the Ninth of Av 5765

בשולי השירים

הזמנה לבכי – בחורף 1973, כמה ימים לאחר שוך הקרבות של מלחמת יום הכיפורים, פרסם ארנון לפיד, מבני התנועה הקיבוצית, את רשימתו "הזמנה לבכי". זו שיקפה את גל הכאב, השכול והיאוש ששטף אז את הארץ. ביני לביני, בכל פעם שדמיינתי את העלול לבוא למתיישבי קטיף, דעתי נטרפה, כנפשי. את החרדות הללו העתקתי אל הבית, בכפר עציון. הרגשתי כי זה הולך להיות "יום הכיפורים" שלנו, של הכיפות הסרוגות.

הארץ הזאת שרועדת – בעיצומו של חורף תשס"ד (2004) פקדה את ארצנו רעידת אדמה קלה שמוקדה היה בצפון ים־המלח. כמה ימים לפני כן חשף ראש הממשלה ברבים את "תוכנית ההתנתקות".

שירים שנכתבו בחול – בחודשים שקרבו לא רציתי לכתוב. שורות, תמונות, דימויים, חזיונות, פסוקי תחנון וקינות באו והלכו אצלי. כמו מעצמם נרשמו. בין היאוש לתקווה, בין החיים למתים, נכתבו השירים בחול. זה החול שלבסוף כיסה הכל. אולי גם את השירים.

In the Margins of the Poems

An Invitation to Cry – in winter 1973, several days after the cessation of the battles of the Yom Kippur War, Arnon Lapid, of the kibbutz movement, published the article "An Invitation to Cry". This reflected the wave of pain, bereavement and despair that swept the country then. Secretly, every time I imagined what was liable to happen to residents of Katif, I went crazy, in my mind as in my soul. These anxieties I transferred to my home in Kfar Etzion. I feared that a "Day of Atonement" was coming for us, the crocheted kipot wearers (the national religious element).

This Land Trembling – in the midst of winter (2004) a mild earthquake occurred in the country, its center was in the northern part of the Dead Sea. A few days earlier the prime minister publicly revealed the "disengagement plan".

Poems Written in the Sand – In the approaching months I did not want to write. Lines, pictures, images, visions, verses of supplication and lamentations came and went, inscribed as though of their own accord. Between despair and hope, between the living and the dead, the songs were written in the sand, the sand which eventually covered everything. Perhaps the poems too.

אני לדודי (מחזור בכתובים)

מה נורא המקום הזה
הלשון נחרבת
כחול ירוק־העין משתבלל
אל תוך עצמו
חוטי שיער אדמוניים נאחזים
בגרגרי זהב המדברות
ורק בת־שחוק נגלית
מן השכיבה העולמית ההיא של גופך היפה
אל סבתי בחלומה

*

הנער מוטל באשר הוא שם.
במדבר רוח אין.
דמו ודם זרעיותיו נמשכים ממנו ואילך.
הוא איננו קורא
אלוהים איננו שומע.

*

הבזקים מהחצר האחורית
תמיד אמרתם לנו שזה עוד כלום. שפעם המתה החצר חיים. בעלי־חיים. בוסתן פירות מגרגר. נשארו עץ התמר והשזיף הגדול. כשהיינו ילדים עוד רקחו מהפירות הסגולים ריבות, ישנו ליקר, והיתר חיכה לנו מבריק ומפתה בקערה הגדולה בשולחן שבסלון. עם השנים לא נותר עוד כוח לטפל ואפילו לקטוף. מדי פעם אמא קוטפת את הסגול־הסגול הזה לשקית ניילון. יש כאלה כבר שעסיסם נוטף, נפצעים בקלות.
פירות רבים מדי שבים אל העפר.

From Me To My Uncle (a cycle in progress)

How awesome is this place
the tongue goes dry
green-eyed blue coiling
into itself
strands of red hair grasped
by golden desert grains
only a smile is revealed
from the eternal lying down which is your beautiful body
to my grandmother in her dream

*

the lad placed where he is
in the desert there is no wind
his blood and the blood of his offspring continue from him onward
he does not call
God does not hear

*

Flashes from the backyard
You always told us this was nothing. That once the yard was full of life. Animals. A gurgling orchard. The date palm and the big plum tree are still here.

When we were kids they still made jams from the purple fruit, aged liqueur, and the remainder waited for us shiny and tempting in a big bowl on the living room table. With the passing years the strength to tend or even to pick became depleted. Occasionally Mom picks the purple-purple into a plastic bag. Some with juice dripping are easily bruised. Too many fruits return to the earth.

*

סבא במרפסת מתקין דבר. צופה בנכדיו, אנחנו, אליעד ואליעז
המשחקים. מעין תחיית המתים.

*

בחלומות עודי עומד בפתח החצר. מציץ לאין־סופה. רואה למרחקים.
שדות שלמים פרושים משם. נהר יוצא ומתפרד.
היום עומד שם, ברב בלוי 29, בניין מגורים.

*

ובלילות
אני נד מהר להר
מתיר את כל העקודים
(ביניהם אתה, אליעזר דודי)
מחפש איילים תמורתם

*

עוד הרהורי צפירה
שכל התקוות הללו יאזלו מן הגוף הצנום
אל אדמתך, סיני?
הרוח עוד חורקת שיניה. אין זה זמן להיעקד. אין הדבר תלוי
אלא בי.
לא היית חייב ללכת. (אני לא הייתי הולך)
היית חייב ללכת. (אולי גם אני הייתי הולך)
חריקת שיני הרוח נדמית עתה לבת־שחוק.
הד הרי־סיני, לו תקרא בשמו!

*

*

Grandpa is installing something. Looking at us, his grandchildren,
Eliad and Eliaz playing. A sort of resurrection of the dead.

*

In my dreams I still stand at the entrance to the yard, glancing at its
endlessness, seeing far, whole fields spread out from there. A
river flows out and splits.
Today, on 29 Rav Blau street, there stands an apartment building.

*

at night
I wander from mountain to mountain
freeing all the bound ones
(among them you, Eliezer, my uncle)
searching for rams to replace them

*

More memorial siren reflections
shall all these hopes drain from your frail body
to your ground, Sinai?
The wind is still grating its teeth. This is no time to be bound. The
matter depends
only on me.
You did not have to go. (I would not have gone)
You did have to go. (Perhaps I too would have gone)
The grating of the wind's teeth now seems like a smile.
Echo of Mount Sinai, if only you would call his name!

*

מחשבה נערית:
לקחת תרמיל גדול,לרדת לסיני,
להפיל עצמי בוואדי הצר,לסדר את גופי פשוט אברים, פנים למעלה,
מבקשות
את זה שלא עזרך,
לא הצילך מחרב פרעה

*

שיחות עם תמונה
החיוך הרך שלך עוד מדבר אלי,
הנה אתה חוזר מן המתים.
אוסף אותי, שעל שמך
אל זרועותיך
אנחנו מסובבים
כל העולם מת
המשא שהיית
הופך לכנף

פרקי המחזור נכתבו מתוך התבוננות מחודשת בדמות
דודי המת, אליעזר פלדמן הי"ד, במהלך תשס"ז,
במלאת חמישים שנים לעלייתו השמימה בגבורה
בקרב המיתלה, מערכת סיני, תשט"ז, ומתוך לימוד
פרקי "המקום" בבית המדרש "קולות" בירושלים.

An adolescent idea:
take a backpack, go down to Sinai,
throw myself down into the narrow wadi,
spread-eagle my body, with face upward
seeking the one who did not help you,
did not save you from the sword of Pharaoh

*

Conversing with a picture
Your soft smile still talks to me,
Look! You are returning from the dead.
You gather me – named after you -
to your arms
we are circling
the whole world is dead
the burden you were
becomes a wing

This cycle grew out of a renewed contemplation of the figure of my dead uncle, Eliezer Feldman, during the year 5767, fifty years after he fell heroically at the battle of the Mitla in the Sinai Campaign of 5716, and the study of my "places" at the Kolot Seminary.

משירי השואה הבאה

*

וְנֵלֵךְ בַּדֶּרֶךְ בָּהּ יָמִים רַבִּים הָלַכְנוּ
הָלוֹךְ וְזָלוֹל הָלוֹךְ וְסָחוֹר הָלוֹךְ
וְסָרוֹר וְסָבוֹא וּמָרֹה וְלֹא נֵדַע כִּי בְּרֶגַע
תִּגַּע אֵלֵינוּ הָרָעָה

*

וְהָיָה בַּיּוֹם הַהוּא אֶשָּׂא עֵינַי אֶל הֶהָרִים
וְאֵין הָרִים
וּכְבָר נָגְעָה רָעָה נָשְׁקָה רַכּוֹת פִּסְגוֹתֵיהֶם נָמַסּוּ נָזְלוּ כְּדוֹנַג הִתְמוֹגְגוּ
גְּבָעוֹת כִּבְקָעוֹת
גַּם רִבּוֹאוֹת הֲמוֹן צִבְאוֹת אָדָם
אֲנָשִׁים עִם נָשִׁים עֲלָמִים וּבְתוּלוֹת זְקֵנִים וָטַף
נָזְלוּ הָיוּ לִנְהַר
הַחֵלֶב וְהַדְּבַשׁ

*

וְהָיָה בַּיּוֹם הַהוּא תָּזוּב הָאָרֶץ מֵחֵלֶב בָּנֶיהָ וּבְנוֹתֶיהָ לֹא תִהְיֶה פְּלֵטָה בְּהַר
יְרוּשָׁלַיִם

*

אוּלַי נָבוֹא, אֲנִי וְאַתְּ, בַּמְּחִילוֹת בְּעֶצְיוֹן
בְּאַהֲבָה שֶׁלֹּא נֵדַע כִּי אַחֲרוֹנָה
פִּתְאֹם, בָּאֶמְצַע, הַתְּשׁוּקָה
תַּעֲמֹד לָנוּ

From Poems of the Coming Holocaust

*

and we shall go the way we went for many long days
glutinous and forth roundabout and forth
and stubborn and drunk and rebellious and we shall not know that
in a moment
the disaster will reach us

*

and on that day I will lift my eyes to the mountains
but there are no mountains
already disaster has touched, brushed lightly, their peaks melted ran
like hot wax hills
dissolved into valleys
the myriad hosts of mankind too
men with women youths and virgins old men and small children
flowed became a river
the fat and the honey

*

and it shall be on that day the land will flow with the fat of her sons
and daughters there will be no refuge on the mountain of
Jerusalem

*

Perhaps we will come, you and I, in the tunnels of Etzion
in a love which, unknown to us, is the last
suddenly, in the middle, the lust
will rise in us

וּבְרֶגַע נִמַּס יַחְדָּו בָּשָׂר וְחֵשֶׁק וּנְשָׁמָה
הַיְלָדִים יָבוֹאוּ אַחֲרֵינוּ

*

וּנְהַר הַחֵלֶב וְהַדְּבַשׁ יָבוֹא יְבַעְבֵּעַ אֶל יְרוּשָׁלֵם הָעִיר
טִפּוֹת־זְהַב־כִּפַּת־הָהָר יָבוֹאוּ בּוֹ בְּאַלְלַי
הַר־זֵיתִים יִזַּל שְׁמָנִים וְשַׁיִשׁ יִבָּקַע בְּאֶמְצָעוֹ
בְּלֹא קוֹל

*

בַּשּׁוֹאָה הַבָּאָה נֵשֵׁב, שְׂרָפִים, עַל הַמִּרְפֶּסֶת
וְנִסְפֹּר יְהוּדִימְנוֹדְדִים

*

כִּי־צִפּוֹר־הַשִּׁיר תֵּחָרֵךְ בִּמְעוּפָהּ וּפִי
הָאָרֶץ יִסָּתֵם מִזַּעַק
חַמָּנִיּוֹת שְׂרוּפוֹת תָּדִיר רֹאשׁ יַרְכִּינוּ
וְיָד יְבֵשָׁה תְּשַׁלַּח הַגֶּפֶן לִפְרֹךְ בְּאֵפֶר
הַשָּׁמַיִם
וְכָל הַחַי בְּזוֹ הָאָרֶץ הַטּוֹבָה
וְהָיָה כֵּאלֹהִים:
תָּכֹל, שָׁקוּף וַאֲוִירִי

and in a moment we will melt together flesh desire soul
    the children will follow us

*

and the river of fat and honey will come bubbling to the city of
    Jerusalem
gold-dome-mountain-drops will come in it in woe
the mount-of-olives will liquefy to oils and marble will split down
    the middle
    without a sound

*

in the coming holocaust we will sit, seraphs, on the porch
    and we'll count the wanderingjews

*

the-song-bird will be singed in flight and the mouth
    of the land will be blocked by screams
burnt sunflowers will frequently bow their heads
and a dry hand will release the vine to crumble in the ashes
    of heaven
and all that lives in this good land
    will be like God:
azure
    crystalline
        ethereal

פּוֹרֵץ הַמַּחְסוֹמִים

לעלי יחיא, מורי מני־אז

עם מינויו לשגריר ישראל באתונה

בְּשָׁעָה מְדֻמְדֶּמֶת זוֹ, לְמַרְגְּלוֹת הַגִּלְבֹּעַ
בְּשָׁעָה שֶׁאֲנִי לְבוּשׁ־זַיִת וְעַל־כָּרְחִי
נֶאֱסָף אֶל שׁוֹמְרֵי הַחוֹמָה
(מֵעֵבֶר הַגְּבוּל גָ'לָמֶה, פַּעַם מַחְסוֹם, פַּעַם
דֶּרֶךְ עוֹלָה מֵעֵמֶק עֲפוּלָה אֶל עֵמֶק דּוֹתָן
וְאֶל דֶּרֶךְ הָהָר וְהָאָבוֹת)
בְּשָׁעָה זוֹ אֲנִי חוֹשֵׁב עָלֶיךָ עַלִי יַחְיָא
אֵיךְ בָּאתָ וְכָל כֻּלְּךָ הַחַם הַכְּרַסְתָּנִי מְגַלְגֵּל אֵלֵינוּ
יַלְדֵי־מִתְנַחֲלִים קְטַנִּים בְּנֵי שִׁבְעָה וְתְ'מָנְיָה בְּאֶרֶץ הַשּׁוֹמְרוֹן הַמִּתְעוֹרֵר
אֶת הַגְּרוֹנִיּוֹת הַמְרַקְּדוֹת
שֶׁל שְׂפַת הַדַּאד.

בְּשָׁעָה מְדֻמְדֶּמֶת זוֹ שָׁבִים בְּנֵי עַמְּךָ, עַלִי, עִם שֶׁבַּשָּׂדוֹת
וַאֲנִי עוֹמֵד לָהֶם מֵעַל לָרֹאשׁ, בְּכָל הַבִּדּוּקִים
וְהַגְּרוֹנִיּוֹת הָהֵן שֶׁבָּאוּ אָז לְפִיּוֹתֵינוּ הַזְּעִירִים
שָׁבוֹת וּמְחַפְּשׂוֹת לָשׁוֹן.

בְּשָׁעָה מְדֻמְדֶּמֶת זוֹ הַכֹּל כִּמְעַט וְאֶפְשָׁרִי
כְּשֶׁלִּבִּי שָׁר עַרְבִית וְיוֹצֵא אֶל הָאִשָּׁה
שֶׁבְּצָלֶיהָ הִתְפַּזְּרוּ מִתּוֹךְ הַשַּׂק לְכָל הָעֲבָרִים
וְאֵיךְ בְּשֶׁקֶט הַגֵּאֶה הַזֶּה שֶׁלָּהּ הִיא מְלַקֶּטֶת וּמְלַחֶשֶׁת
אֶחָד מִן הַשִּׁירִים
שֶׁלִּמַּדְתָּ אוֹתָנוּ עַלִי יַחְיָא מִכְּפַר קַרַע בְּאֶלְקָנָה הַבְּתוּלָה הַנִּבְנֵית

The Barrier Crasher

FOR ALI YICHYA, MY TEACHER
ON BEING APPOINTED AMBASSADOR IN ATHENS

At this dusky hour, at the foot of Mount Gilboa
when I am dressed in drab against my will
to join the guards of the roadblock
(the Jalama border crossing, at times a roadblock, at times
  a road ascending from the Afula Valley to the Dotan Valley
    and to the road of the mountain and the Patriarchs)
at this hour I think of you Ali Yichya
  how you came all warm and paunchy rolling to us,
little settler-children of *Sabaa* and *Thamania* in the land of waking
    Samaria,
  the dancing gutturals
  of the tongue of *Thad.*

At this dusky hour your people are returning, Ali, the people that are
    in the fields
and I stand in their way, with all the security checks
and those gutturals that came then to our little mouths
Return searching for a tongue.

At this dusky hour almost anything is possible
  when my heart sings Arabic and goes out to the woman
  whose onions have spilled out of her sack all over the place
and how in her proud silence she collects them whispering
  one of the songs
that you taught us Ali Yichya from Kara Village in the virgin Elkana
which is being built

[וְלֹא יָדַעְתִּי שֶׁשָּׁרָשִׁים לְךָ וּלְכִפָּרְךָ בְּגִבְעוֹתֵינוּ
שֶׁתֵּל־אָבוֹת שֶׁלְּךָ שֶׁנֶּעֱזַב בְּאֶחָד יוֹם־אֶל־גֻ׳מְעָה לִפְנֵי
מִיתֵן שְׁנִין (מָצְאוּ בַּתֵּל סִיר בָּשָׂר וַעֲצָמוֹת עָזוּב עַל פֶּחָמִים)
סָמוּךְ וְנִרְאֶה מֵאֶצְלֵנוּ]

בְּשָׁעָה מְדֻמְדֶּמֶת זוֹ אֲנִי רוֹאֶה אוֹתְךָ עֲלִי יַחְיָא
    נוֹשֵׂא בְּדֶגֶל הַטַּלִּית
בִּמְרוֹמֵי מוֹשַׁב אֵלֵי יָוָן שֶׁבָּאַקְרוֹפּוֹלִיס
    וְאֵיךְ בְּנֶפֶשׁ־עַרְבִי־הוֹמִיָּה מְאַחֶה אֶצְלִי אֶת כָּל הַחֲתָכִים
        בַּנֶּפֶשׁ הָאַחַת

כָּאן בַּמַּחְסוֹמִים יוֹרֵד עַכְשָׁו הַשֶּׁקֶט
    וְרַק זְהַב־קְלִפּוֹת־הַבְּצָלִים־שֶׁנֶּאֶסְפוּ עוֹד מְגַלְגֵּל רֵיחַ
        הַשִּׁיר הַהוּא וְרֵיחַ
מְבוּכַת הָאִשָּׁה וְהַחַיָּל שֶׁמֵּעָלֶיהָ
        (הוּא אֲנִי)
וְאָנָא מֻשְׁתָּאק־לַכְּ יָא סִיד עַלִי

בְּשָׁעָה מְדֻמְדֶּמֶת זוֹ, לְמַרְגְּלוֹת הַגִּלְבֹּעַ
    עוֹד מְעַט יִפֹּל הַיּוֹם עַל חַרְבּוֹ
וְעֶרֶב כָּחֹל־קוֹבַּלְטִי יַעֲלֶה
        מִבְּלִי יָרֵחַ.
מִגֶ׳נִין הַיָּפָה וּבְנוֹתֶיהָ שׁוּב יִסְתַּלְסֵל הַשָּׁמַיְמָה
    הָאַלְלַהֻ אַכְּבַּר בַּמָּקָאם הַמֻּפְלָא
    וַאֲנִי אֲשַׁלַּח אֶצְבְּעוֹת כֹּהֵן עִבְרִי
        אֶל אֲהוּבַי שֶׁבֶּהָרִים
        וְגַם אֵלֶיךָ

[and I didn't know that you and your village have roots in our hills
that your ancestral mound which was deserted on an *el-juma* day
miten snin ago (they found in the mound a pot of meat and bones
        left on the coals)
near enough to be seen by us]

at this dusky hour I see you Ali Yichya
   carrying the prayer shawl flag
in the heights where the Greek gods of the Acropolis dwell
   and how in an excited-Arab-soul all my cuts are healed
        in the one soul

here at the roadblock silence descends now
   and only the gold skin-of-gathered-onions still broadcasts a smell
        that song and the smell
of the embarrassment of the woman and the soldier standing over her
        (meaning me)
and *ana mushtak- lak ya sid* Ali

At this dusky hour, at the foot of Mount Gilboa
   soon the day will fall on its sword
and a cobalt blue evening will rise
        with no moon.
From pretty Jenin and her daughters once again will curl skyward
   the *allahu akhbar* in the wonderful *mak'am*
      and I will send fingers of a Hebrew Priest
         to my loved ones who are in the mountains
            and to you as well

קַו רֶכֶס אַחֲרוֹן

בַּקַּו הָרָכוּס לְמוּלִי
עַרְבִיּוֹת קְטַנּוֹת רְכוּנוֹת
כְּאִלּוּ כּוֹרְעוֹת לָלֶדֶת
גֶּפֶן חֲדָשָׁה

בַּקַּו לְאַחֲרָיו
מוֹסְקִים בַּחֲבָטוֹת מַקֵּל דַּק
זַיִת קַדְמוֹן וְסָדוּק

בְּקַו רֶכֶס אַחֲרוֹן
כּוֹרַעַת אֲהוּבָתִי שֶׁלִּי
אִשָּׁה יְהוּדִיָּה גְּדוֹלָה
מְלַקֶּטֶת שִׁבְרֵי קוֹצִים
שֶׁנָּשְׁרוּ מִבְּשָׂרִי

אֵינֶנִּי רוֹאֶה
אַךְ יוֹדֵעַ
בְּקַו רֶכֶס אַחֲרוֹן

The Last Ridge

On the ridge opposite me
small Arab women are hunched
as though squatting to give birth
to a new grape vine

On the following ridge
thrashing with thin sticks they are harvesting
an ancient cracked olive tree

On the last ridge
my love squats
a great Jewish woman
gathering broken thorns
that fell from my flesh

I don't see
but I know
on the last ridge

*

בֵּין בְּתְרֵי הָאוֹטוֹבּוּס וִיהוּדֶיךָ
הַשְּׂרוּפִים אֲנִי כּוֹרֶתֶת עִמְּךָ בְּרִית לֵאמֹר:
לְזַרְעֲךָ נָתַתָּ, זַרְעֲךָ שֶׁיְּסַפֵּר וְיִמָּנֶה מֵרֹב
עוֹנִים וַחֲרוֹנִים
כַּכּוֹכָבִים הַנִּדְלָקִים לִפְנֵי נְפִילָתָם
(וּמִי יוּכַל לָשֵׂאת הַמִּשְׁאָלָה)
לְזַרְעֲךָ שֶׁהוּא עַכְשָׁו זָקֵן שׁוֹכֵחַ מִשְׁקָפָיו
(הַמֻּנָּחִים לוֹ עַל חָזֵהוּ אוֹ מִצְחוֹ)
וְלֹא יוּכַל לָשׁוּב אֶל הַהֶסְכֵּם אוֹ אֶל
דִּבְרֵי הַמַּחֲזֶה הָהֵם

בֵּין בְּתְרֵי הָאוֹטוֹבּוּס אֲנִי כּוֹרֶתֶת עִמְּךָ בְּרִית לֵאמֹר:
אַל תְּשַׁחֵט אֶת הַצִּפּוֹר

*

Among the fragments of the bus and your burnt
Jews I make a covenant with you saying:
to your seed you gave, your seed who shall be counted and numbered
according to the multitude of suffering and wrath
like stars ignited before their fall
(O who will be able to bear the wish)
to your seed now an old man forgetting his glasses
(which are on his chest or his forehead)
and unable to return to the agreement or to
those words of the play

Among the fragments of the bus I make a covenant with you saying:
do not slaughter the bird

מְחַכִּים, עֲדַיִן

"ואנכי הסתר אסתיר פני ביום ההוא"

(דברים ל"א)

(בהשראת "מחכים לגודו", סמואל בקט)

מְנַסִּים, עֲדַיִן, לַחֲלֹץ אֶת הַנַּעַל.
מְנַסִּים לִזְכֹּר מַפַּת־הָאָרֶץ בִּצְבָעִים.
זוֹכֶרֶת?
טוּרְקִיזִים שֶׁל יָם הַמָּוֶת הַמְתִּיקוּ לָנוּ פַּעַם, בַּלֵּילוֹת.
הַמָּקוֹם הַזֶּה, הָעֵץ, הַקָּהָל הַמְגַחֵךְ בַּחֹשֶׁךְ
נְתִיבֵי־מִלּוּט בְּרוּרִים מְאֹד: אַחֲרֵי־הַקְּלָעִים מִשְּׂמֹאל
אַחֲרֵי מִיָּמִין.
מְחַכִּים. אוֹתוֹת בָּאוּ וְהָלְכוּ וּבָאוּ, עִנְיָן שֶׁל מַזָּל,
הַחְלָפַת כּוֹבָעִים, גּוֹרָל עִוֵּר.
וּמְחַכִּים. כָּל יוֹם, וּבְדִיּוּק יָתֵר: רֵאשִׁית עַרְבּוֹ שֶׁל יוֹם
לְיַד הָעֲרָבָה הַבּוֹכִיָּה שֶׁכָּלוּ דִּמְעוֹתֶיהָ.
שֶׁיִּתְגַּלֶּה, שֶׁיֹּאמַר מַשֶּׁהוּ, מַה בְּדִיּוּק בִּקַּשְׁנוּ אוֹתוֹ –
מִין תְּפִלָּה, אֵיזוֹ תְּחִנָּה בִּלְתִּי־מֻגְדֶּרֶת
מְסַפְּרִים שֶׁהוּא אָמַר שֶׁהוּא יֵרָאֶה
מְדַמִּים בְּכָל אִוְשָׁה לְעוֹד־מְעַט, הִנֵּה
לוֹכְדִים שַׁעֲשׁוּעֵי יוֹמְיוֹם וּמוֹצְצִים מִיצֵי־צִבְעֵי־עוֹלָם
מֵעַל קוֹרוֹת דַּפָּיו (הַלְּבָנִים, אֱמֶת)
וּמְחַכִּים.
לֹא עוֹד מְסוֹבְבִים כִּכַּר שֶׁל מוֹשִׁיעִים קְדוֹשִׁים
בְּחֵיק עַצְמֵנוּ אֲחוּזִים
אוּלַי צוֹפִים לַחֲשֵׁכָה מֻחְלֶטֶת, בָּהּ נֵרָאֶה

Waiting, Still

"And I will hide my face from them on that day"
(DEUTERONOMY 31)

(After Samuel Beckett's "Waiting for Godot")

Trying, still, to take off the shoe.
Trying to remember the colored map.
Remember, dcar?
The turquoises of the Dead Sea turned sweet for us once, at night.
This place, the tree, the audience giggling in the dark
very clear escape routes: behind the wings on the left,
on the right.
Waiting. Signs came and went and came, a matter of luck,
changing hats, blind fate.
And waiting. Every day, very punctual: the start of the day's eve
near the weeping willow whose tears have ceased.
He should reveal himself, should say something, what exactly did we
ask of him –
a sort of prayer, some undefined supplication
they tell that he said he would see
we imagine with every murmur that soon, look
we are capturing everyday amusements and sucking juices of the
world-colors
off of the events of his pages (the white, truth)
and waiting.
No longer circling the square of holy saviors
held in our own lap
perhaps peering at the absolute dark, in which we will be seen

בֵּינְתַיִם שְׁלַל רִקְמָה בָּרְקִיעִים, נוֹטֵף מִתְּהוֹמוֹת
כְּמִשְׁי סִין, כְּמוֹ חָבוּר
מַרְקִיד מַדְאֶה אֶל עֵבֶר קֶדֶם מַאֲדִים, כְּמוֹ לֹא יוֹדְעִים
שֶׁמֵּאָחוֹר דּוֹהֵר הַלַּיְלָה וְקָרֵב עַד שֶׁאוֹרֵב אֶל
רֶגַע לֹא נִצְפֶּה, אוּלַי סִיבוּב נוֹסָף מִסְּחְרוּרֵי הַוַּלְס
בּוֹ נִלְפֶּת סְכוּרֵי־עֵינַיִם מִפָּנָיו, וְהוּא, מֵאַחֲרֵי לַגַּב
אֲזַי זוֹנֵק

אָז מְחַכִּים. אִי אֶפְשָׁר מִכָּאן לָלֶכֶת, רַק עַל חֶבֶל דִּמְיוֹנִי
(אִם לֹא נַרְפֶּה מִשָּׂא הַחֲבִילוֹת מִשְּׁנֵי צִדֵּינוּ)
וְגַם הַזְּמַן מִתְעַתֵּעַ, לֹא יוֹדֵעַ
אִם פְּעִימוֹת שָׁעוֹן בַּכִּיס אִם לֵב
עַד בּוֹא הַנַּעַר הָרִאשׁוֹן, הַמְּפֻחָד
וְעַד לֶכְתּוֹ
וְעַד שׁוּבוֹ לְמָחֳרָת

נוֹשֵׂא בְּשׂוֹרַת אָדוֹן הַמְּסָרֵב לְהֵרָאוֹת
הַיּוֹם, אֲבָל מָחָר בָּטוּחַ שֶׁיָּבוֹא
וְהַמָּחָר, הַמָּחֳרַת הַזֶּה, הוּא בֶּאֱמֶת סִפּוּר חָדָשׁ
כְּמוֹ אַתְחַלְתָּא
נִצַּת אָבִיב וְעֵץ שֶׁמִּתְחַדֵּשׁ בְּעַלְעַלָּיו
וְגַם אֲנַחְנוּ שְׁנֵינוּ נִתְעַבֵּר אוּלַי
בַּצִּפִּיָּה שֶׁיֵּרָאֶה
שׁוּב מְחַכִּים. שִׂמְחַת הַיַּחַד מְכַסָּה, כְּמַעְיָן הַמִּתְגַּבֵּר
עַל כָּל קוֹלוֹת מֵתִים
כְּמוֹ כְּנָפַיִם, חוֹל, עָלִים
מְמַלְמְלִים, מְרַשְׁרְשִׁים, מְמַלְמְלִים
כְּמוֹ נוֹצוֹת, עָלִים וְאֵפֶר

meanwhile there is a rich tapestry in the sky, dripping from chasms
like silk of China, as though joined
dancing gliding toward a reddening east, as though unaware
that the night is galloping behind, approaching in ambush
an unexpected moment, perhaps another turn of the waltz's pirouettes
in which we cling tightly, our eyes dammed against it, and he, behind my back
leaps then

So we wait. Impossible to leave here, except on an imaginary rope
(if we don't lighten the load of the bundles on both our sides)
and time also deceives, I don't know if the ticking is the watch in my pocket or the
heart
until the arrival of the first frightened youth
and till his leaving
and till his return the next day

bearing news from a lord who refuses to show himself
today, but will surely come tomorrow
and tomorrow, the next day, is truly a new tale
like a beginning
a spring bud and a tree renewing itself with leaflets
and the two of us also will be pregnant perhaps
with the expectation of his appearance
waiting again. The joy of togetherness covers, like a fountainhead,
all the voices of the dead
like wings, sand, leaves
mumbling, rustling, mumbling
like feathers, leaves and ashes

עַד שֶׁאֵין יוֹתֵר מִלִּים
נוּ, מְחַכִּים. מַעֲנִיקִים לַעֲרֵמוֹת גְּוִיּוֹת הַמַּחֲשָׁבָה
הָרִים שֶׁל מַשְׁמָעוּת, לֹא מַפְסִיקִים
לְנַסּוֹת, לִתְפֹּשׂ תְּנוּמָה, לְצֵל שֶׁל חֶסֶד אַחֲרוֹן
אוּלַי בַּגּוּף
לָשׁוּט
כְּצֶמֶד נְשָׁרִים מֵעַל לַיְשִׁימוֹן הַזֶּה
לָחוּשׁ בָּאֲבָרוֹת מַשָּׂא הַגּוֹזָלִים
עֲקֵבוֹת שֶׁל רֹךְ־אַדְנוּת, מַלְכוּת
לָעוּג עוּגַת שָׁמַיִם הַגְּדוֹלִים
וּלְהָעֵז כִּמְעַט לָגַעַת

כִּי מְחַכִּים. וְאוֹרְרִים, כְּהֵרָיוֹן שֶׁלֹּא נִגְמָר
אֶת יוֹם הַיּוֹם, אֶת יוֹם מָחָר
וְעוֹד שָׁרִים, רוֹקְדִים, מְגַלְגְּלִים
מַה שֶּׁנִּשְׁאָר, מִקְּצֵה מִדְרוֹן
וְשׁוּב שָׁבִים וּמְטַפְּסִים. בַּקּוּרְנָסִים
וְנֶחְבָּקִים וְנֶחְנָקִים וְנִשְׁנָקִים וּמִתְנַשְּׁקִים
וְנֶחְבָּאִים עַד פַּעַם יְחִידָה, מֵאַחֲרֵי הָעֵץ
אֲשֶׁר בַּגָּן

מִפְּנֵי הַזֶּה שֶׁשּׁוּב לֹא בָּא.

until there are no more words
nu, we are waiting. Granting to the piled up corpses of thought
mountains of significance, not ceasing
to try, to catch a nap, for a shadow of a final benevolence
perhaps in the body
to drift
like a pair of eagles above this wasteland
to feel in the pinions of burden the fledglings
traces of gentle rule, monarchy
to encircle the great heavenly sphere
and to dare almost to touch

because we are waiting. And cursing, like an unending pregnancy
today's day, and tomorrow's day
and yet singing, dancing, rolling
what remains, from the end of a slope
and again returning and climbing. With claw hammers
bear-hugged and strangled and suffocating and kissing
and hiding until an only time, behind the tree
that is in the garden

from him who once again will not come.

*

וּבַלֵּילוֹת
כְּשֶׁאַתְּ נִפְרֶשֶׂת לְפָנַי כְּמוֹ מְנִיפָה
אַשְׁמִיעַ לָךְ קוֹלוֹת הִתְעוֹרְרוּת
וּנְהִי וְקִינָה
וְכַמָּה שֶׁאַתְּ יָפָה
וְאֵיךְ נִוָּתֵר חֲבוּקִים לְיוֹם אַחֲרוֹן
וְשׂוֹחֲקִים

*

and at night
when you are spread out before me like a fan
you will hear my arousing cry
   and a lamentation and a dirge
and how beautiful you are
and how we will remain in an embrace to the end of days
      laughing

*

וּכְשֶׁאֶהְיֶה קָרוֹב אֶל מוֹתִי
הַנִּיחִי אוֹתִי אֵצֶל
שְׂדֵה הַחַרְדָּלִים
וּבוֹאִי אֵלַי, כָּךְ
כַּפַּיִךְ בְּכַפַּי
וּפִיךְ עַל פִּי
וְעֵינַיִךְ עַל עֵינַי
אֶעֱצֹם

*

when I am close to my death
   leave me by
   the wild mustard field
and come to me, so –
your hands in mine
   and your mouth on mine
   and your eyes on my eyes
      I will close

לאחוז בציצית ראשו של הזמן, ולטלטל

ניסיון לומר משהו עם השירים

כיצד כותבים שירה כשמסביב הכל שותת?

"אם העיניים פקוחות יותר מדי", כותב גנסין באיגרת לברנר, "הבה ונעצום אותן בכוונה", ואפשרות זו של עצימת העיניים מפתה כל העת, מפתה.

לא ניסיתי להמתיק הימים בשירים. משהו בי ציווה להיות פָּקוּחַ – בעיני הבשר כמו בעיני הרוח – אל ליבת הזמן הבוער הזה.

בחבלי המלים נעקדו יחד אֶרוֹס ותָנָטוֹס, קִטרוג ואמונה, אירוניה ופאתוס, כיסופי־משיח ואפשרויות של יאוש – משמשים בערבוביה, כרוכים זה בזה.

אורי צבי גרינברג הצהיר פעם: "אנוכי ארנין את המלה 'פוליטיקה'". מעיד אני על עצמי שמים וארץ, כי לפואטיקה שכָּנַסתי בזה הספר כמעט שאין דבר עם הפוליטי. יש כאן ניסיון אישי מאוד להיות אחד עם העצב הזה החשוף של "הגורל היהודי".

חלק מן השירים כמו אנוסים היו להיכתב. וכבר יכול הייתי לזהות בפחד שהתכדר אצלי בבטן את רגע עיבורו של שיר חדש. כמובן, כדרכם של שירים, רבים מן העוּבָּרים הללו לא נולדו עד הֵנה.

ועכשיו, בעוֹברי שוב בין השורות שנאספו לכאן, עולה לפנַי זכרם הטוב של שניים ממורי ורבותי שנקראו לישיבה של מעלה בשנים הללו: יהודה עמיחי ונתן יונתן. סימנים שמסרו לי בחייהם ובשיריהם פועמים באותיות.

"עבדי זמן – עבדי עבדים הם", כתב רבי יהודה הלוי, ואני ביקשתי להפוך עצמי מעבד־עבדים לזה שאוחז בציצית ראשו של הזמן, ומטלטלו.

אליעז

To Grasp Time by the Hair and Agitate It

An attempt to say something about the poems

How to write poetry when around you all is bleeding?

"If the eyes are too open," writes Uri Nisan Gnessin in a letter to Brenner, "let us close them on purpose." The possibility of turning a blind eye is always tempting, so tempting.

I did not try to sugarcoat the times with poems. Something inside ordered me to turn a watchful eye – a physical eye as well as a spiritual one – to the core of this burning time.

The cords of the words bound together eros and thanatos, accusation and faith, irony and pathos, longing for the Messiah and the possibility of despair – all intermingled, convoluted.

Uri Zvi Greenberg once declared: "I shall elate the word 'politics.'" I testify before heaven and earth that the poems I have collected in this book have almost nothing to do with politics. There is here a very personal attempt to be at one with the exposed nerve of "the Jewish fate."

Some of the poems were written as though by their own force. From the fear collecting in my belly I could readily identify the moment the embryo of a new poem began. Of course, poetry being what it is, many of those embryos have not reached birth until now.

And now, returning to the lines collected here, there comes to mind the blessed memory of two of my teachers who have passed on to a better world: Yehuda Amichai and Natan Yonatan. Signs I received from their lives and from their poems are pulsating in the letters.

"Those who serve time are servants of servants,'" wrote Rabbi Yehudah Halevi, and I have attempted to change myself from a servant of servants to one who grasps time by the hair and agitates it.

Eliaz

Notes

"News"

Kisufim, a Kibbutz in the Negev, gave its name to the roadblock which controlled traffic to and from the Gaza Strip on the road which was the site of frequent terrorist attacks against Israeli citizens. The word *kisufim* means yearning.

"Tashlich"

Tashlich is a prayer recited on the Jewish New Year while facing a body of water. It expresses the wish to be rid of one's sins by casting them into the water.

The *chatzav* is a common wild flower in Israel. It blooms at the time of the Jewish New Year. The tall white flowers that sprout from its bulb are the first sign that autumn is approaching.

"Kislev, On the Way To Hebron"

Kislev is the Hebrew month corresponding approximately to December. During Kislev the portions of the Torah relating the stories of the Hebrew Patriarchs who spent their days in the Mount Hebron region are read in the synagogue. The poet, who lives in this region as well, sees the image of the Patriarchs in his Arab neighbors.

The 19th of Kislev is celebrated in Hassidic circles as the Festival of the Liberation of the Hassidic Master Rabbi Shneur Zalman of Liadi from prison. He was incarcerated for fifty-three days after being falsely accused of treason. It is also the anniversary of the death of the Rabbi and poet Moshe Zvi Neriah, who would wake his students in the morning (Eliaz Cohen among them) with the "Yidelach" song.

"With Me From Lebanon"

Havdala is a prayer recited on Saturday night at the closing of the Sabbath. It marks the passage from the holy Sabbath to the secular weekdays when the speaker may make coffee. Instant coffee is referred to colloquially as "nes," (from Nescafe). The Hebrew word נס (*nes*), meaning miracle, leads the speaker to ask what place miracles have in his situation. A literal translation was not possible. Instead I translated the idea that the mundane act of preparing instant coffee led the speaker to contemplate his situation with all its horrors.

4th of Iyar,which falls in May, is the date of the Memorial Day for Israeli Soldiers who died defending their country. It is immediately followed by Israel's Festive Independence Day. The year 5760 corresponds approximately to 2000, the year in which the Israeli Defense Forces pulled out of Lebanon.

"Palestinian Passover":

Rais, meaning "the head," was a common epithet for the Palestinian leader Yasser Arafat, signifying that he was the authentic leader of the Palestinian people. The poem was written in the midst of the second intifada, in which Arafat was confined to his headquarters by the Israeli military.

"On the second day":

The date is that of the Shavuot festival on which, according to tradition, the people of Israel experienced a divine revelation when the Torah was given to them on Mount Sinai.

"Nablus We Have Returned To You":

In the heart of ancient Nablus lies the grave of Joseph, son of the

Patriarch Jacob. According to tradition Menashe and Ephraim, the sons of Joseph, are buried there as well. On the Jewish New Year 5761 (September 2000), when the violent disturbances of the second Intifada began, the Druze Israeli soldier Madchat Yuseph was wounded while defending the site of Joseph's grave and bled to death because it was impossible to send medical aid.

"Poem On Tel and Not Aviv"
The name Tel Aviv is composed of two Hebrew words: *tel*, meaning a man-made hill covering the remains of an ancient settlement and *aviv*, meaning spring. The name represents the idea of a modern Israeli city in the ancient land of Israel. Tel Aviv was actually suggested as a Hebrew translation of the title of Herzl's *Altneuland.*

"Poems Above Ariel":
Written while serving in the military reserves, when the poet returned as a father and a fighter to the scenes of his childhood in western Samaria near the settlers' town Ariel. "Ariel," according to tradition, is also one of the names of the city of Jerusalem. Starting from the 1990's the town has attracted many new immigrants from the former Soviet Union, among them Christians for whom local churches have been established.

"My brothers poets of Palestine" – here the poet addresses the noted Palestinian poets Fadua Tuqan and Mahmoud Darwish.

"biladi min dam umin roch" – fragments of slogans and songs of the militant Palestinian uprisings.

"Kifl-Hares" a Palestinian village near Ariel which, according to Arab tradition, is the site of the grave of Joshua son of Nun.

"and suddenly spring burst forth"
Marcheshvan, or Cheshvan, is the month in the Hebrew calendar which follows the joyous fall holiday season (approximately corresponding to November). "Mar," meaning bitter, was added to its name because it lacks the festiveness of the previous month.

"The Bound Ones":
Gush-Halav and Masada – two of the strongholds of the great Jewish rebellion against the Romans in the Galilee and Judah in 66–74 C.E.

"Selling Again":
Geneve – relates to the Geneva initiative in which the Israeli negotiators decided to relinquish their rights to the Temple Mount, the Jewish nation's most holy site, and to leave the Tower of David, which is actually the turret of a mosque belonging to the Ottoman fortifications of the wall of ancient Jerusalem.

"This Land Trembling Under Our Feet":
The concept *"tsumud"* requires a member of an Arab tribe to have uncompromising loyalty to his land.

"The Barrier Crasher":
"The barrier crasher" was a legendary maneuver of the Israeli forces in their War of Independence in 1948. The poet, on military reserve duty, is stationed at a roadblock in northern Samaria where he sketches the possible harmony between the Hebrew and Arabic languages and the peoples who speak them.

"The tongue of Hadad" – a term for the Arabic language which stresses the pride that its speakers take in its comparative richness, particularly of tone

ana mushtak- lak Arabic phrase meaning "I yearn for you."

"Me To My Uncle":
The Hebrew title *ani ledodi* is taken from *The Song of Songs* where the meaning is I am my beloved's. In modern Hebrew *dod* means uncle, while the allusion suggests the additional meaning of beloved.

Hebrew dates

The following are approximate equivalents of the Hebrew dates that appear in the poems:

Months	*Years*
Kislev – December	5708 – 1947–1948
Iyar – May	5760 – 1999–2000
Shevat – February	5761 – 2000–2001
Nisan – April	5762 – 2001–2002
Iyar – May	5764 – 2003–2004
Sivan – June	5765 – 2004–2005
Av – August	

The Jewish calendar year begins in mid-September.

About the Author

Eliaz Cohen

Eliaz Cohen is a leading figure in the contemporary renaissance of religious poetry in Israel. Born in Petach Tikva in 1972, he is the author of four collections of Hebrew poetry, and an editor of the poetry journal *Mashiv Haruach*. In 2006, Cohen was the recipient of the prestigious Prime Minister's Award for Literature and the Avichai Sabbatical Prize. In recent years he has stood out as a social activist dealing with such issues as religion and state, the socio-economic gap, and the sanctity of life. He grew up in Elkana and lives with his wife and four children in Kibbutz Kfar Etzion.

The fonts used in this book are from the
Garamond & FrankReal families